"This book can serve as your personal care[...] job-seeking books focus on career choice an[...] age your career upwards. With his experienced-based, innovative [...] tricks,' Meshriy propels you beyond the limits of your personal career boundaries to create a new way of thinking about yourself, your job, and your future."

> —Robert C. Chope, Ph.D., author, *Dancing Naked: Breaking Through the Emotional Limits That Keep You from the Job You Want*, and Professor of Counseling at San Francisco State University

"It doesn't matter whether you're working for a corporation or for yourself—you need to evaluate your career track on a regular basis. *Thinking Outside the Cubicle* covers career assessment with practical examples and exercises that can be used at all stages of your career. Included here are elements usually forgotten by career self-help books, including an understanding of the psychology of the worker in a social group and how to value everyone's unique contribution to the workplace."

> —Catherine Marshall, CEO, California Association for Microenterprise Opportunity (CAMEO)

"In writing *Thinking Outside the Cubicle*, Meshriy, the quintessential career counselor, has effectively combined his extensive business experience with his passion for helping people be true to themselves at work."

> —Sheila Weisblatt, Momentum Career Consulting, San Francisco, CA

THINKING OUTSIDE THE CUBICLE

HOW TO CHANGE THE JOB YOU HAVE INTO THE JOB YOU WANT

NORMAN J. MESHRIY, M.S., Nationally Certified Career Counselor

NEW HARBINGER PUBLICATIONS, INC.

Publisher's Note

This publication is designed to provide accurate and authoritative information in regard to the subject matter covered. It is sold with the understanding that the publisher is not engaged in rendering psychological, financial, legal, or other professional services. If expert assistance or counseling is needed, the services of a competent professional should be sought.

Distributed in the U.S.A. by Publishers Group West; in Canada by Raincoast Books; in Great Britain by Airlift Book Company, Ltd.; in South Africa by Real Books, Ltd.; in Australia by Boobook; and in New Zealand by Tandem Press.

Copyright © 2002 by Norman J. Meshriy
New Harbinger Publications, Inc.
5674 Shattuck Avenue
Oakland, CA 94609

Cover design by Amy Shoup
Cover image by Chip Simmons/Getty Images/FPG International
Edited by Carole Honeychurch
Book design by Michele Waters

ISBN 1-57224-267-1 Paperback

Printed in the United States of America

New Harbinger Publications' Web site address: www.newharbinger.com

04   03   02

10   9   8   7   6   5   4   3   2   1

First printing

Contents

A Tribute   v

Introduction   1

PART I

Using Your Uniqueness to Your Best Advantage on the Job   **5**

Values Assessment: What Motivates You to Action? 🗁 Use Your
Introversion to Get Ahead 🗁 Use Your Extroversion to Get Ahead 🗁 Use
Your Past Failures and Successes 🗁 How Can You Get Out of Your Own
Way? 🗁 Shift from Job Security to Self-Security 🗁 Capture Your Ideas 🗁
Balance Your Life and Your Work

PART II

Getting the Most Out of Your Job Right Now   **39**

What Do You Need and Want? 🗁 Troubleshooting Workplace Problems 🗁 Make Some Changes 🗁 Make a Move 🗁 People Who Make Your Job Hell 🗁 Creating Good Work Relationships 🗁 Downsizing Your Workload 🗁 Money Talking 🗁 Keep Your Job Exciting 🗁 Listening to Your Inner Dreamer

PART III

Moving Forward in Your Job   **83**

Where Do You Want to Go from Here? 🗁 What Passion Skills Can You Offer? 🗁 Your Twenty-First Century Skills 🗁 Networking: Walk Around Research 🗁 Honing Your Interview Skills 🗁 Looking Down the Road: Creating Goals 🗁 Taking the First Step to Put Your Plan in Action

A Tribute

The first book I read in the field of career management was *What Color Is Your Parachute?* by Richard Nelson Bolles (Ten-Speed Press: Berkeley, CA, 2001). Richard first published this book in 1970 but has faithfully kept it current through its multiple editions over the past thirty years. Richard has been one of my heroes ever since I entered the field of career counseling. I have always wanted to write a book, and Richard's easy style and common sense approaches made me feel that, when I was ready, my book would happen. The time has come and here is my book! Thanks for being a wonderful role model for me, Richard. Your wonderful books and your equally wonderful presentations at the many national and international career profession conferences have made you one of the best-known and most renowned professionals in our field. I have talked about you with so many of our colleagues, I know you are an inspiration to many, many thousands of career counselors throughout the world.

—*Norm Meshriy*

Introduction

Are you employed and actively involved in your job but longing for the sense of fulfillment you always dreamed you'd find in your career? If so, you're definitely not alone. Many people languish in unsatisfying jobs, assuming that they don't have the skills or opportunities to have a fulfilling work experience. But making a change is well within your grasp, and *Thinking Outside the Cubicle* provides the tips and tricks you'll need to shift into satisfaction—right now, today. So, dive right in. The book is divided into three parts, and each part will challenge you to take actions that will help you along your career path. Each part begins with a chapter that takes you through an assessment that provides a framework for all that follows.

Part I provides avenues for you to explore some unique facets of the person you are. You have traveled through life developing your own very unique style and determining key values that are important to you. You may not realize it now, but you demonstrate your style and value in everything you do. *Thinking Outside the Cubicle* will guide you to assess these values, making these broad decision parameters of your life more visible to you. You will be invited to explore various aspects of your personality and approach that can be extremely powerful or may get in your way. You will be reminded of the tremendous learning available to you through both your successes and failures. You will see that you can provide your own security, make use of your unique insights, and gain balance in your life and your work.

Part II provides techniques and tools for making the most of your job. You will take a needs assessment, troubleshoot your work issues, and see many creative ways that you can make changes in your compensation and the situations and relationships of your work life.

Part III takes you on a trip into the future. You will assess your plans and skills while learning techniques for moving forward in your career.

As you read, you may notice that a major theme of this book is "You are the key." The elements of the uniqueness of who you are provide your keys to success. Your creativity about the situations of your life and your willingness to try out new approaches will yield vast treasures. Acknowledging your deepest motivators and confidently asserting your ideas and your plans will mold your present and your future in very satisfying ways for you.

Another major tenet of this book is the importance of making your vision, mission, issues, plans, ideas, and dreams visible for early awareness and focused action. In the exercises, you will be invited to do a lot of writing, preparation, and planning and then move to implementation. Preparation is as important as the actions you take, and writing provides a magical tool that allows you pre-thought, prevention, and a platform for action. Writing is also a source for reflection, revision, and proof of movement. The written word can provide a very powerful record of success and failure for continual growth and learning.

Feel free to open the book to any chapter that appeals to you, as each is written to stand on its own. You'll also need to get a journal, notebook, or pad of paper to write on. Each chapter contains ideas, tips, and techniques for new ways to approach the elements of your worklife. Each new insight you find in this book is aimed at improvement of your situation today. You will reflect some on the past, take action right now, and move to plan and protect your future. You are the focus of this book. You can do a lot with the variables of your world, but your action is the key. Start today.

PART I

Using Your Uniqueness to Your Best Advantage on the Job

You are the person you are because of the life you have led. Your life has been unique. No one else in the world today or in the centuries of mankind has had your life experience. You have an absolutely unique perspective on the world. Utilize your uniqueness! Make your mark on the world. Part I guides you to take an introspective look at yourself, reminding you of the strength of who you are.

You have a unique set of values that apply directly to your work life, things that are very important to you. You can explore these values in "Values Assessment: What Motivates You to Action." You have an introverted nature or an extroverted nature that can provide clarity about the strengths and preferences you have for situations and activities. Explore these aspects of yourself in the second and third exercises in this part of the book. And don't be surprised to find that you can relate to both! Extroversion and introversion are not absolutes. You have elements of both, but an inclination toward one or the other. Familiarity with this inclination will provide valuable self-knowledge and understanding.

You learn from every situation that occurs—it doesn't matter if you experience the situation as bad or good. The potential for learning and growth is available from every situation. "Use Your Past Failures and Successes" explores this point and demonstrates that even the most challenging problems you've experienced have contributed to your growth.

The beliefs you carry may need to be challenged. Some of them may get in your way and impede your success. "How Can You Get Out of Your Own Way" shows you some of the ways that you might get in your own way.

The next exercise, "Shift from Job Security to Self-Security," invites you to make a paradigm shift from searching for security from "outside" sources to seeing the power you have to provide your own security through your development and assertion of who you are. Promoting this "self-assertiveness" is carried forward in chapters 7 and 8 as you have the opportunity to capture and implement your own insights and recognize and assert your uniqueness to achieve balance with your life and your work.

You are unique. Take the time to reflect on your singularity. The strength and power you will derive from this reflection will be invaluable to you in directing your career. Enjoy this exploration. Self-exploration may seem selfish or self-absorbed on the surface, but it is perhaps the most generous activity you could undertake. You need to take care of yourself as a primary concern in life, and when you take good care of yourself you are in better shape for everyone else in your life. The one person you cannot escape in life is yourself—wherever you go, there you are!

Values Assessment:
What Motivates You to Action?

Have you ever taken stock of your values? Although your values play a part in every decision you make, you may not give them much conscious thought. Your values have developed gradually over the course of your life and are based on your experience. Always there, but often unnoticed, values represent what is important to you in your life, what gives your life meaning and relevance. They provide an inner framework of how you make choices and are your deepest motivators. Taking stock of your values can bring them into the foreground and help you make more mindful decisions about what you truly want and need from the world of work.

If I followed you around and watched how you behave, I could discern some of your values. I could see how you treat people. I could see where you spend time. I could take note of the activities that bring you joy and relaxation. I could see what interests you have. If I notice that you are a good listener, that you tend to reflect back what people tell you so that they are encouraged to speak more about something important to them, I might see the value you assign to helping others, of being of service to others. If I see you lost in a project that requires your mechanical skills, your abilities with things, I might be seeing the joy you get and the value you assign to your physical being, your physical skills. But I'm using my own words to explain my view of your values. You might speak differently about the things that I see. The language of values is unique to the individual. If seven people in a group are asked to define a particular value, each of the seven will have a different and distinct way of describing the meaning of the value to them. Values are as unique as the individual!

Take variety as an example of an important value selected by several individuals. Variety for Charlene is "variety in tasks; doing different things; new challenges, activities, learning opportunities." In speaking about the value she puts on creativity, Jennifer says "I want to use my mind in a creative fashion. There is always room for new ideas, ideas to help make things better, faster, and more efficient." Michael describes the value he puts on creativity in this way, "I want to use my creativity, to sing, draw, play the piano, act, write poetry and short stories—I am an artist with atrophied muscles."

Each of us has a set of parameters that we've developed over the course of our lives. We get these parameters from our families, from our work, from the events of our lives, and from the people with whom we have shared our lives. Our descriptions

Advancement	Fast Pace	Mental Creativity
Adventure	Feelings	Movement
Artistic Creativity	Five Senses	Physical Challenge
Caregiving	Genuineness	Power/Authority
Challenging Problems	Help Others	Precision Work
Change	High Earnings	Public Contact
Community	Humor	Risk
Competition	Imagination	Security
Decision Making	Independence	Spirituality
Entertain/Perform	Intellectual Stimulation	Time Freedom
Entrepreneur	Intuition	Unlimited Earnings
Environment	Knowledge	Variety
Excellence	Leadership	Work Alone
Expertise	Location	Work with Others

of our values are unique, as unique as our lives.

Here is a list of forty-two values:

1. From this list, pick out about eight of your most important values.

2. With this subset of the original list, ask yourself two questions: "What does this value mean to me?" and "Why is this important to me?" Write your answers in your journal or notebook.

3. Once you have the answers to these questions, take this information through one more transformation—into statements that begin with the word "want" or "need." This list of *want* and *need* statements provides you with key parameters for future decisions.

   Example 1: George describes *independence* as "to be able to do what I want to do, when I want to do it, with little or no supervision for the performance of the task." He sees this as very important to him because "I enjoy knowing what is required and being allowed to use my own ideas and creative solutions." From these answers to questions about the value of independence, George crafted the statement, "Want the independence to determine how to complete a project—to be given a job, the constraints, and to be able to make the decisions, layout my plan, and deliver the results."

   Example 2: Amy describes *security* as "a job and salary that I can depend on." Amy says she needs to know that she can meet her financial obligations. She needs to have enough money so that she does not have to worry, as such worry detracts from her ability to be creative and to enjoy life. From the descriptions of what this value means to Amy and why it's important, she crafted the statement, "Need to know that I will have a job, that my skills are marketable, so that I need not worry about money."

4. Keep this list in a safe place, a place where you will see it from time to time and be able to reflect on its importance and be better able to integrate these values into the world around you.

With conscious awareness of your values, you may find that you begin asking for things to change in ways that would better suit you. Your decisions may seem easier to make, and your vision for the future might be clearer.

Use Your Introversion to Get Ahead

If you are a quiet, private person by nature, you may believe that you're not as competitive as the fast-talking, quick-on-their-toes, outgoing, interactive type of person. As someone who has counciled hundreds of successful introverts, I'm here to tell you that this belief simply isn't true. There is a lot of power inherent in your introverted style.

Introverted people tend to get their energy from within. If you are more the introvert:

- ☺ you are more quiet and reserved by nature.

- ☺ you are more comfortable in the world of thoughts and ideas and less comfortable in the outer world of people and things.

- ☺ you need to take in information and develop it to some level of depth and understanding before putting out your own thoughts.

- ☺ you find being alone a time for reflection and recharging.

- ☺ your introverted style is more introspective and reflective, and you will need to think before speaking or taking action.

This is the introverted way, and this style can be every bit as successful as the more outgoing, interactive types.

Robert works for a major restaurant chain and is looking to take a more administrative position with the company. He wants to begin overseeing a number of individual restaurants and providing leadership to the managers of these locations. He was at first upset when his Myers/Briggs (a widely accepted personality test) assessment indicated a strong inclination to introversion. Robert has been in the restaurant business for over thirteen years, has managed restaurants, interacted with all the restaurant staff, acted as host to the patrons of the restaurant, and basically taken charge of all facets of restaurant business. Robert had his own, somewhat negative opinion of more introverted people—he found them to be too shy, too quiet, and alone a lot of the time. Robert did readily admit to being kind of shy, somewhat quiet, and he does enjoy spending time alone to reflect and recollect himself.

As we discussed the qualities of the introverted style, Robert began to see some of the things about himself that he takes for granted. He could see how he uses his depth of concentration, so much a part of the introverted style, to understand the financials of the restaurant and to deal with the details of the menu, the schedule, and all the processes and procedures of the business. He began to see his depth of concentration as a great asset. Robert told me he is willing to do presentations, but needs a lot of time to develop the presentation, study the material, and internalize the information necessary for his delivery.

Robert said that other people often want him to give them an instant response, but to respond in the moment is something he finds difficult. Robert is very quiet in the first part of meetings; he is thinking, assessing, taking in the information of the meeting and doesn't speak immediately because things have not crystallized for him as yet. When Robert does speak, he delivers a very thoughtful response, a deeper look at the issues at hand, or something that no one has yet identified. The people on his team respect his quiet, thoughtful approach.

The strengths of the introvert include depth of concentration, reflection, comfort with the world of ideas and thoughts, and often a delayed response that is more thoughtful. All of these traits can contribute to success. Weaker areas for the introvert in executing their role will show in responding in the moment, delivering verbal presentations quickly, selling and marketing, and networking. For all of the weaker areas, there are developmental strategies for the introvert that will produce more effective results.

Four Problem Areas and Tips for Success for the Introvert

Problem 1 Your quiet, introverted style may keep you from selling and marketing your good results to others. People may be unaware of your good results and you may miss out on opportunities that would be great for you.

Tip *Sell and market in your own way.* The introvert is more effective one-on-one and with small groups. Set up situations that allow you to talk and work with people in ways that are more comfortable for you so that others see you at your best. Turn your depth of concentration loose on developing statements about your results or other information that lets others know what you can do. Selling and marketing for the introvert is a lower-key exercise requiring pre-thought, planning, and preparation. As people in your organization get to know and trust you, your strengths will come to mind and you'll move up.

Problem 2 You may avoid important meetings and events so that you can stay in your comfort zone. This could keep you less visible and less available to new opportunities.

Tip *Get out of your comfort zone.* Make a strong effort to attend meetings, make arrangements to meet with people, and attend events in which networking can occur. Visibility is very important inside and outside of organizations, but is not a natural habit for the introvert. You will need to focus on attending, participating, and seeing that you are invited—looking for opportunities to become more visible to those you want to impress. Watch people who seem more graceful in a crowd—often observation is a great learning technique for the introvert.

Problem 3 You may shy away from opportunities to let people know what you know. Important people in your department or your company may never be aware of your contribution and your potential.

Tip *Get out in front of people and speak your craft.* Look for opportunities for presentation. The introvert takes subject matter to depths, and such deep understanding can help you develop exceptional presentation material. The introverted person can be as powerful a speaker as the extrovert, but the style of preparation will be distinct. The introvert will deliver with confidence and strength when the preparation has been thorough, when they have achieved comfort with the subject matter, and when they've anticipated questions and interaction.

Problem 4 You may not prepare for a meeting, attempting to rely on spontaneity. This is not a very good introvert strategy and could lead to embarrassment. Speaking in the moment may be more difficult for you, given your introverted nature.

Tip *Take time alone to prepare for a public session where your input and participation will be necessary.* If you are more introverted by nature, relying on your spontaneity will not serve you. Taking time to prepare in some way for the content of the meeting by doing some research, reading, calling some of the participants and discussing issues, or asking other knowledgeable people about the relevant issues will provide some level of preparation. These strategies help you take advantage of your introverted nature to develop ideas and insights so you can go to the meeting well prepared and confident. Preparation will help you enhance your level and quality of participation and will encourage you to speak up at important moments.

    The introverted style can be very powerful, but only if you're aware and mindful of the strengths and weaknesses of this style. With mindful awareness, you can take advantage of the strengths of the introverted way and take advantage of strategies for minimizing or improving areas where you're less able. Remember that the introverted style is just an inclination you have—it is not absolute. You have the ability to develop more extroverted qualities if you wish, but you will need to mindfully undertake this development.

Use Your Extroversion to Get Ahead

There are many ways in which people who are more outgoing by nature seem well-suited to business and industry. There are other aspects of your job that call for quiet, introspective work or call upon your depth of concentration. Some of this work will always be there for you, and it provides opportunity for development and growth. Too much quiet, solitary work might provide an indicator that you might be in the wrong job and headed for difficulty. What are some strategies for dealing with these less comfortable requirements for the extrovert?

If you are more extroverted by nature, you're very attuned to the outer world of people and things. In fact, as an extrovert you tend to receive energy from interaction with others, moving about, taking action, and speaking your thoughts. From a business point of view, this sounds like an excellent tendency. The more extroverted among us will no doubt meet more people, take in more situations, be more socially bold, and generally have greater potential for the visibility to help a business grow. There are many ways in which people who are more outgoing by nature seem well-suited to business and industry.

Mary has been in office situations for over twenty years. Her jobs have always called upon her depth of concentration, her ability to be accurate with accounting and numbers, and her writing skills. But Mary is more extroverted by nature. Her performance evaluations over the years have tended to focus in on her liabilities. She's often made errors with detail and has been reprimanded for talking too much with others, for moving about the office, for speaking up too quickly. The one thing that she really enjoyed about her work and an area of very positive contribution was the contact she had by phone with people in other parts of the company. She really came to know all of the people in her branch and in all of the satellite units of the company, gaining familiarity with their families and other personal aspects of their lives. Mary craved recognition for the good quality relationships she had built and maintained.

Mary worked with a career counselor to rediscover her strengths and now is planning to move into the retail sales part of her company and serve people directly. It turns out Mary loves the clothes and designs that make up the product line for the company. She has a great deal of confidence in her ability to combine clothing to out-fit a person and she loves to do this for many of her family and friends. Mary dreams of being of service in this way, helping people with their selection of just the right piece of clothing or the "look" they are seeking.

The extroverted style is most advantageous in a job that calls for an outgoing personality. Mary had some aspects of her work that called for her extroversion, but this extroverted work was not the predominant part of her job. She will be happier and receive more recognition for her innate abilities in a job more designed to take advantage of her comfort interacting with people.

Five Problem Areas and Tips for Success for the Extrovert

Problem 1 You may blurt out a response that could have been better crafted, or quite possibly, should not have been said at all.

Tip *Before you reply, take a moment to ask yourself, "Could I use more time before I respond?"* Often taking a little time to think about an issue can provide the reflection necessary to tailor your response, to not hurry decisions, and to allow for a more thoughtful reply. Sometimes a comment like "I see...," or "yes...," with a little silence after the word or the phrase will invite additional thought and ideas from the individual with whom you are speaking. If you deliberately take a break from the conversation and dedicate some time to thinking more in depth about the topic, you may be surprised how differently you view the issue.

Problem 2 For meetings in which you need to participate, you may rely too heavily on your extroverted ability to help you operate "on your toes." This tendency could have the effect of making you seem ill-informed or not interested to others.

Tip *Get out of your comfort zone—schedule time to take an issue apart, alone, or with a trusted colleague.* Deliberately scheduling time to take an issue apart could be a tremendous new technique for you to build skills that are less natural to you. This technique could yield more in-depth understanding and insight that you could not attain otherwise. With more pre-thought, the facets of the problem have a chance to crystallize for you, giving you a higher probability of more sophisticated discussion and results.

Problem 3 You may be tempted to put a few notes together and then stand and deliver a presentation without thorough preparation. This is especially true if you have a very outgoing personality with a very spontaneous component to your natural approach. This approach can yield spontaneous disorder, too much concentration on less important ideas, the potential to say things that are not well thought out, and may result in poor delivery.

Tip *Take the time to craft a presentation before you stand and deliver.* Go ahead and write out what you want to say so that you can "craft" the ideas, the concepts, and the facts. Rehearse the presentation, taking time to translate written word to spoken word. The purpose of rehearsal is practice, not memorization. When you deliver this presentation, you will be much more in command of the information, more attuned to your audience, and more relaxed and spontaneous.

Problem 4 You may tend to dominate the discussion, causing others to feel shy about sharing their ideas. This could have the effect of making others in your team feel left out and leave the team missing outstanding input from others.

Tip *Do something to remind yourself that you want to avoid jumping in as soon as an idea comes to you.* My client Stephan moves his chair back from the table a bit when he wants to control his propensity to jump in with his ideas. When you hold back a bit you may be surprised by the dynamics of the group and the additional participation of others. Along with encouraging others' input, you may in fact find yourself listening and enjoying more when you do not feel you have to carry so much of the load of the meeting.

Problem 5 Your extroverted nature could cause you to develop quantity, not quality in relationships. You may not take the time with individuals to establish deeper relationships that could foster two-way support and development.

Tip *Take more time with individuals to develop more intimate relationships.* Networking is more natural to you because of your outgoing, interactive style. The more extroverted will tend to meet a greater number of people, but will spend less time with each person. If you go out of your way to spend more time with someone, and invite more one-on-one experiences, you have the opportunity to develop more long-term, enduring relationships. These relationships are a very powerful contributing force to repeat business, referrals, and advertising of your product or service.

The extrovert sometimes needs to do work that calls for action and interaction with others. If you are mindfully aware of the need to develop skills to allow you to do the more solitary, in-depth work requiring attention to detail, you will be more successful accomplishing such tasks. The extrovert will be more successful in roles and responsibilities designed to take advantage of their innate abilities. If you job does not make enough use of your extroverted qualities, look for ways to enhance your responsibilities through activities that involve others. Take opportunities that will allow you to represent your organization, speak publicly, interview others, and participate on cross-functional teams.

Use Your Past Failures and Successes

As you look back on the story of your life and career, do you ever feel regret for a decision made, an action taken or not taken, something in your past that seems to come back to haunt you from time to time? Just about everyone has a few key events or periods in their lives that make them cringe or recoil when they spring to mind. These bumps in the road don't have to cause nothing but regret, however. Believe it or not, they can actually be cause for celebration.

You have learned from every situation you have ever encountered, and you can tell a very interesting story of success or learning from all that has come your way. You are more interesting because of your challenges, demonstrating a unique strength through your tales of success, and your humanity and balance in your tales of dealing with adversity.

Ben abused drugs and alcohol for a good part of his life. In middle age, he was fired from a very good job and began moving from job to job, taking what was available and using his physical abilities in many seemingly unrelated jobs.

Through the years, Ben had a vague idea that he was good at listening to others and offering them guidance, but he'd never considered doing work that would make use of these natural listening skills. His dependence on drugs and alcohol kept him from deep personal understanding.

As Ben ended his dependence on drugs and alcohol, an interest in using his more natural talents began to grow. He began to recognize the value of his ability to help people and took steps to make use of this ability in his work. He continues in his present work, doing carpentry and helping people with their home improvement needs, but he also has completed a counseling training program and provides drug and alcohol counseling for teens. The counseling training has given Ben new tools with which to work with others and helped him to hone his listening skills. Ben receives a lot more appreciation these days from his carpentry clients for his interest in and solutions to their needs. He also gets enormous satisfaction from working with the teens, a target population for which he has a great deal of understanding and empathy.

Ben has successfully changed his beliefs about the period in his life he considers a major bump in his road. He was able to take some valuable lessons from that period that he had once considered a total loss. Ben now gets a lot of satisfaction out of living his life using these lessons that could only have come from overcoming great adversity.

Linda is a very introspective individual who has learned the value of taking understanding from difficulties in her professional life. Linda is operating in a very senior role in her company, the most senior position of her career. She has access to all the executives of the company, including the president. Many difficult situations happen in this very dynamic company, and Linda finds her role as head of human resources to be quite challenging. She has many successes, but also some things that give her a feeling of failure. Senior position hiring decisions made without her awareness, and having to deal with the explosive anger of executives, are examples of bothersome situations in which Linda seeks more a graceful execution of her role.

Linda keeps track of all of her successes and failures in her journal. She is a highly motivated individual, always on the lookout to improve her understanding, her performance, and her comfort with her job. She talks about her experiences, shares successes, and makes the most of learning opportunities that come from the bumps in the road. With such a positive spirit and willingness to take risks and grow, Linda has achieved good results and a great deal of recognition over the past two years.

Exercise: Capture Successes and Failures

1. Carry a notepad with you for a week and capture little bumps in the road that occur.

2. Do not miss the opportunity to also capture successes. You may even be able to relate some of the successes to bumps that occur. *Analyze each of your successes to determine if there was some setback that occurred before success was achieved.*

3. Analyze each bump in your road to see if you can turn that bump into something positive, some learning opportunity, a new way to look at the situation.

Reframing your outlook about painful events can change your life, turning your bad experiences into a source of wisdom. You may tune out the potentially incredible revelations that come from difficult experience, but you really grow when you can listen to the great messages that come from both positive and negative experiences. You can learn as much, if not more, from difficulties as you can from your successes. You may not even be aware of the learning you are receiving. Your successes and your failures have contributed to the uniqueness of your being. When you take the time for a deeper look at your results, it's possible to take deep learning, growth, and determination from your experiences.

How Can You Get Out of Your Own Way?

You may be your toughest critic. You may be your worst enemy. There are beliefs you have that may not be true. There are natural preferences that you have that may not be optimum for the situation at hand. Operate as you always have and you may not move forward. Operate with new vision, try out new approaches, take some risks, and watch out—you may feel a growth spurt and accelerated progress.

The workplace is a wonderful venue for experimentation and positive change. Sometimes the greatest changes you can make are those changes you make "inside" by looking at things differently and making mindful choices. What comes through you naturally is not always the best for your job or your career.

Allen was a procrastinator. He had learned that he is more apt to take action and make progress when he is under some kind of pressure. So Allen developed a habit of waiting for the urgency to build on a project or task and let the adrenaline kick in. But Allen realized that he was not always successful and often risked being late. To take advantage of his natural tendency, Allen devised a plan to break down jobs into component pieces that he would then schedule for completion. By setting his own small deadlines, Allen began to generate his own urgency and found that he was able to create a little of his own "adrenaline rush."

Joan wanted to please everyone and was uncomfortable when someone in her universe was upset or distressed. As a result of her concern for the comfort of those around her, Joan tended to take on a lot of issues and found herself frequently interrupted and burdened with too much to do. Joan decided to develop successful ways of dealing with her nature and began to train herself to say things like "I don't have the time right now, but perhaps we can talk over coffee later." This was at first very difficult for Joan—new approaches are often uncomfortable and awkward. But soon Joan found herself more in control of her time, able to focus more on her work, and when truly necessary, she was more available to others. She found others respectful of her needs and she naturally developed a very kind way of avoiding taking on issues from others.

Jean had a tendency to rely on his gut instincts and did not let the facts get in his way. If you gave Jean a little information, he was convinced he had the situation under control. Jean was right much of the time, but found there were critical times when his intuitions were off, leaving him embarrassed. Jean decided to add preventive thought to his approach and tried to insert mindful questioning of his instincts. When he could catch himself making a leap to a conclusion, he would ask, "What are the facts at hand?" This question would cause Jean to take a little time to ask some questions or seek some factual basis for his conclusion. Jean still valued his gut instinct as much as in the past, but with preventive thinking, he moved forward with more confidence.

Lorreta managed her projects very closely, directing the steps of the plan, the schedule, and making certain that all was accomplished by the appointed date. Lorreta was first to speak in team meetings, was constantly tracking down status information, and was very visibly upset when things went wrong. Lorreta listened to coaching advice and began to use techniques that were quite scary to her. She would state a pressing problem at a team meeting and ask for input from others. She found that her team enjoyed the process of brainstorming and each member began to take on more responsibility and ownership. When she gave up trying to control every little thing, Lorreta found her job much more enjoyable, worried less, and was able to concentrate her efforts on supporting her team and working on the real tough issues. Lorreta's team began to appreciate her more, volunteered information to allow her to track progress, and worked harder and longer to meet their shared schedule.

Common Stumbling Blocks

Here are some other areas in which people tend to get in their own way.

- ☺ You keep feelings inside until you are about to burst. When you finally let the feeling out, it has grown and become explosive. Your expression of the issue/concern involves primitive behavior—yelling, screaming, and carrying on in ways that embarrass, scare, or anger others.

Strategy: Practice being more aware of your feelings. Keep notes in a journal about how you feel and test out ways of expressing feelings in objective, constructive ways. Talk at first to people you trust about your feelings and the actions you anticipate taking, seek advice from people that are more comfortable in expressing feelings.

⊕ You are too organized. You get very upset when things change and you're required to change plans or operate spontaneously.

Strategy: Recognize that change is inevitable. Build flexible plans that anticipate change. When change happens, embrace it by looking at it as an opportunity to grow and develop. To the degree that you accept change and develop new coping skills, you will find yourself less stressed with change and more successful.

⊕ You are too trusting. You believe people when they say they will do something and are disappointed and surprised when they do not come through.

Strategy: Practice developing new techniques for keeping people on track with their commitments to you. With enough lead time for recovery, send an e-mail as a follow-up to your conversation. As reminder, get back in touch with the individual to see how things are going. You will find that your follow-through will need to be more rigorous until you get to know a person's style and the amount of trust you can place in them.

⊕ You are too self-critical. You want excellence in everything you undertake. You can always find fault with your accomplishments, and you always see the flaws in your work.

Strategy: Recognize that you are a bit of a perfectionist. There are things in your job that you must do to a high degree of excellence. But for other tasks, you may run into trouble if you don't allow yourself some slack. Have your team or someone you trust provide criticism of your product to help you gain objectivity. This will help you prioritize where your energies should really be going.

⊕ You tend to consult with people with whom you share similar approaches and similar ideas.

Strategy: Open up to the possibilities. Seek out diverse opinions to invite new, unique perspectives on a situation, a presentation, a product, or a solution to a problem. Ask a colleague in a different setting, ask a vendor, ask your child, ask a customer, ask on a helpful forum on the Internet. Make it your business to get a wide variety of input.

 Exercise: What Keeps You Stuck

1. Write down a project that you want to move forward, a relationship you want to develop, visibility you seek, recognition you want.

2. Ask yourself and write down your answer to the question: "What characteristic of me could be a contributing factor to my lack of success?"

3. Ask yourself and write an answer to the question: "What new approach could I take that might provide an avenue to success?" *You may need to call upon the advice of someone you know who is more effective in such situations to offer you insight into successful navigation strategies for this situation.*

Shift from Job Security to Self-Security

You are the CEO of your own business, whether you work for someone else or for yourself. If you always think of what you do in this way, you will be inclined to take more responsibility for making your way, ensuring your results and actions are visible, and being certain that you are recognized, fairly compensated, and valued for who you are.

Most people look for security from an "outside" entity like an organization. An organization can provide benefits, growth opportunity, good work, a paycheck, and a place to go each day. Looking for security from within is a paradigm shift, a concept that many are embracing and finding more powerful than anything we believed in the past that an employer could provide. You can have self-security whether you reside inside an organization or provide goods and services from outside of organizations. Self-security is a mindful strategy you can choose that can positively alter your perception of your situation.

Over the course of time, your relationship with organizations has changed. In the not-too-distant past, you were encouraged to stay with an organization for the duration of your career. You had a career with a company and expected to advance "up the ladder" of the organization. Some award programs in the past were triggered by years of loyalty and time in position. It is far more customary today to have award programs targeted strictly on results and accomplishments. You will need to keep your skills sharp, looking for security to come from your marketability, your continued ability to meet the needs of the organization, and your ability to meet your own needs.

The messages you receive from organizations today tell you that you are the master of your own destiny, and that you will be rewarded for your contributions for as long as you can meet the needs of the organization.

Elizabeth works for an architectural firm. She has a degree in architecture and has worked for over six years in the field. She became concerned about the lack of progress she was making in attaining more creative design work. Her skills were highly regarded, and she was a very trustworthy employee, but still the kinds of assignments she wanted would not come to her.

Through her work with a career counselor, Elizabeth confirmed that her interest, skills, personality type, and values are all well-served in architecture, and she knew that she enjoyed being part of the development of structures designed with the needs of the environment in mind. Elizabeth also discovered she expected others would recognize her talent and select her for the work she wanted to do.

Elizabeth came to realize that she had been reluctant to express her desires and make her own way. She had lived through several layoffs and was still hurting from treatment by a bad boss. Elizabeth began to put things in place to take control of her career. She began a program of tests to gain professional certification in the State of California, and she began asking for assignments to directly assist designers and to work with specific people to gain new skills. Elizabeth became much more bold in expressing how she wanted to develop in her career. Very shortly after a discussion she set up with her boss, she was given an assignment to help out on a major design effort. Elizabeth says, "I need to rely on me and stop looking to others and the organization too much."

Four Key Elements of Self-Security

Skills focus: A real focus on skills and self-development is a main tenet of self-security. You can become more secure through understanding, articulating, and continually developing your skills and abilities.

Self-Management: In today's economy, organizations are "flatter," having fewer layers of management. Leadership skills are required in every position. You will need to plan your work, communicate the status of your work, identify problems and resources required, coordinate your work with others, achieve results, and take credit for your accomplishments.

Networking: You will need to be in connection with others with whom you can talk over issues, strategies, plans, and receive and give support. The quality of your relationships and connection with people in and out of your industry, organization, occupation, interfacing jobs, or jobs of similar skills can provide for contribution to your self-security. Strategies could include reaching out to others in your own workplace, joining professional associations, searching the Internet, reading journals and other publications, and taking classes.

Lifelong Learning: Another tenet of self-security is commitment to lifelong learning. The feeling that you know what is happening in your industry and in your area of work is important to your sense of security. No longer can you be complacent with your knowledge and approach. Technology and continuous improvement methodologies are enhancing quality and levels of sophistication in all aspects of work and life.

Exercise: Self-Security

What is the one action you can take in the next week to enhance your self-security? Is there an area of skill that you could develop that would enhance your marketability? Are there people with whom you could network that could provide industry, company, trade, or other insight? Is there an important professional relationship that you could strengthen or rekindle? Is there an association that you have been tempted to join, but have not taken the action to join?

Write down the action you choose to take next week and make a commitment to see it through.

It is imperative that you continue to develop and keep aware and connected. Sharpening skills and knowledge and developing your network and self-management techniques are keys to your enduring success.

Capture Your Ideas

You have the ability to take all that is innate to you and all you have learned and use it in a creative way. You are capable of putting together all of the information available to you and coming up with insights, flashes of intuition that provide unique views of situations, problems, decisions, new ideas, new inventions, and new concepts. Your insights will be triggered by events in your life and your work and can provide you with ideas to make your experience richer and more satisfying.

These ideas often come to you when you're in relaxed state. Walking alone, standing in the shower, driving in your car, listening to music, in the midst of a stimulating conversation, or when you are brainstorming with others, an idea can pop up when you least expect it. Somehow your creativity is awakened and produces a flash of inspiration. If you take the time to recognize and record the arrival of your ideas, you can develop or enhance an ability that can provide a powerful tool for you in taking more control of your work and your life.

Everything you use, almost everything you see that is made by humans, came from inspiration leading to ideas. Of course, some ideas are better than others, but all of your insights carry the possibility of providing you with messages from your deeper self, expressions of your own consciousness and subconscious, the things that matter to you, another dimension of your uniqueness, and, finally, terrific new ideas.

Hans gets ideas about mechanical things. He envisions physical solutions to manufacturing problems. He has become a consultant to various companies in the Silicon Valley of California. The insights that Hans has tend to relate to mechanics, physics, and robotics. Hans is forever writing in his notebook, making schematic drawings, and doing calculations. He tells me of his need to carry this notebook with him at all times because he never knows when an idea will come to him.

Some people are very talented in the world of ideas about others, and their inspirations are naturally about relationships, interactions between people, and their feelings. **Jill** receives insights about the people she knows, the people with whom she comes in contact, the people she observes, and the potential future situations of people. Jill keeps a journal that she simply calls "People."

Sandy is an artist who tends to get inspirations by watching things over time. Her observation skills are very well tuned. She sits out on the balcony of her home and watches the shadows of the clouds as they move over the hills, creating shapes, colors, textures, and designs. She then captures the ideas born from these inspirations in her paintings. She keeps a sketch pad with her almost all the time because she never knows when she will see something that gives her a new idea, a new look, or a new concept for her paintings.

You may get a lot of new ideas, so many that you are not able to even take note of them. Or, you may receive only a few of these insights, so few that when asked, you can hardly remember an example. Everyone has insights and ideas, but the conditions and the content of inspiration will be as different and unique for you as they are for Hans, Jill, and Sandy.

You will need to capture these ideas in some way, or like the dream, they will slip away, perhaps never to return. Some carry a notebook in their pocket, purse, or stuck to the dashboard of their car to record ideas. Some use tape recorders that allow them to speak out their ideas for later transcription. There are also devices that allow for the recording of ideas in the shower. The small, hand-held computers and telephones with ability to store information are making it easier and easier for you to record your ideas for later evaluation and perhaps implementation. Over time, with enough experience, it is possible for even your simplest ideas to come to sophisticated fruition, but you will never know the potential of your ideas if you cannot capture them. And the more you capture and implement these ideas, the more self-expression and control of your situation you will feel.

Work provides an excellent venue for trying out new ideas. Maybe your idea is one that can be implemented by you or by others in the workplace. Some ideas allow for immediate implementation; others will take careful planning and coordination.

Exercise: Insight Capturing

Take some time this week to keep track of the ideas that come to you while at home, during travel, at work, while exercising—anytime. Find some convenient way to keep a notebook, a computer, or a tape recorder on hand to use as soon as an idea reveals itself to you. Think about the possible uses of each of your ideas, how you might develop an idea, and what you might do to test out the idea.

1. Write down one idea that you can implement or test out at work.

2. What is the first step you will take to implement this idea or test it out?

No one in the universe can have the absolutely unique perspective that you have. The ideas you receive through this extraordinary ability you have to uniquely experience and express all of the wisdom and knowledge of your being can be invaluable. If you capture these ideas, you can try implementing them to extraordinary benefit. By bringing your ideas to reality you will have a greater sense of self-expression, agency, and best of all, you will be giving of your own uniqueness to the world.

Balance Your Life and Your Work

Work demands often seem to compel people to push their lives into the background and to put most of their energy and time into their jobs. But you don't necessarily have to find yourself stranded on a work-related island. There are strategies for keeping aware of other aspects of your life so that you can achieve more of a balanced outlook and allow more humanity into your work experience.

You spend a lot of your time on the job. Potentially, you will spend most of your awake hours in work of some kind. And even when you are not at work, your mind may be working on the problems and situations of your workplace. You are conscientious, you want to succeed. Work provides a lot of what you need for life. But work doesn't have to become you *whole* life. It is important for you to develop a level of balance in your life that incorporates your work, but does not allow your work to take over.

Frank had a very demanding sales-management job and began to feel that he was simply "going through the motions." After getting some coaching, Frank implemented a "Balance Plan" that helped him to approach his work in very different ways. Frank began to share more of himself with those he could trust in his workplace. He began to talk more of his family and things that interested him personally, and began to relax more at work. Outside of work, Frank would share more of his work strategies, successes, and frustrations with his trusted friends and relatives. A key to his Balance Plan was openness and genuineness. Another major key to the plan was monitoring its results. Frank identified a new level of comfort in his professional life with no detriment to his accomplishments at work. His team hit 115 percent of their goal during the first six months of Frank's experiment, and he received appreciation from all of those around him for his relaxed, comfortable style.

Irene always felt that she had to maintain a very professional, no-nonsense approach to her marketing role. At work, she felt like she had to wear a façade, a mask. She felt like a different person when she left work, but had little energy by the time she got home. Work was taking all of Irene's energy. She decided a career change was in order and went to a career counselor.

Through her experience with the counselor, Irene began to see that her career was not the issue—it was more her own approach to her work that was the factor contributing to her distress. Irene implemented some changes to her approach that had immediate benefit. She began working from home at least one day a week to attend to detail work. She brought in some pictures of her family, artwork, and began scheduling lunch, walks, and stretching times as strategies for balance. Irene was surprised by the warm discussions these changes generated. Her co-workers appreciated her more personal style and found that when she took the time to take care of herself, she was a better colleague. Irene began to enjoy her work more and began to find other clever ways to integrate her life and her work.

Many who lose their jobs and can afford a little time before actively pursuing their next job feel quite differently about their lives after only a few weeks following job loss. Some of these people express and demonstrate:

- ☺ Increased enjoyment of the time with their family and friends

- ☺ Interest in the mundane tasks of shopping, house cleaning, talking with the neighbors, and completing projects around the house

- ☺ Time to attend to health issues including more focus on the quality of meals, scheduling exercise and stretching

- ☺ Taking time to think about the long-term career aspirations, ideas for projects, training, and/or business development

- ☺ Getting back to areas of interest like sports, crafts, musical pursuits, the arts, collections, reading, or writing

- ☺ Rekindling of memories and getting back in touch with old friends, former colleagues, and relatives

By using some simple strategies to bring more balance into you life, you can allow yourself to reconnect with some of these neglected aspects of your life and bring more of yourself into your workplace as well.

Exercise: Balance

1. Write down three things that are very important to you (*color, music, art, family, activities, environmental issues, animals, reading, writing, spirituality, etc.*)

2. For each of these items write down a way that you can integrate this aspect of you into your work situation (*color your cubicle/workspace, decorate with pictures, books, interesting items*).

3. Write three ways in which you can share your work, your professional aspirations and your work strategies with those you trust.

4. Write one way that you can increase time available to you for your life outside of work (*negotiate to be able to work from home, leave a bit early or come in a little late, allow yourself time during the day for a walk, a lunch, or a break to talk with someone about something fun*).

You have the ability to add a bit of depth to any part of daily life, depth that provides meaning and connection. With a little creativity, you can make very small changes that can provide very powerful integrative forces. Put balance in your life and your work and you will find more satisfaction and fulfillment.

PART II

Getting the Most Out of Your Job Right Now

You have more power than you might suspect to control the variables of your life and your work. Have you ever asked for what you want in your work? Have you explored the many creative options for making change to the situations of your work? These are two of the many powerful methods that most people never use to improve their satisfaction at work.

You can initiate changes that could make monumental difference to your perception of your situation and the quality of your worklife. With new technologies, new trends in the world of work, new approaches to relationships, potential new learning and certification, and positive assertion of your own desires, you can cause very positive change to happen, clearing your path for progress, growth, and success.

Determine your needs in the exercise "What Do You Need and Want?" Troubleshoot workplace problems in the following exercise. Begin the exploration and assessment of changes you could orchestrate in the remainder of the chapters of this section. In "Listening to Your Inner Dreamer," you will be encouraged to think about your workplace dreams in preparation for the future planning you will find in the final part of the book.

What Do You Need and Want?

Your job is busy. You probably have so much to do that you can never seem to take the time to think about your job in its entirety—there are too many little pieces that require your attention. It may be the time for you to take a careful look at your job. There may be small things that you can do to make a big impact on your day-to-day work schedule that can provide for more happiness and enhance the degree to which your job allows you expression of who you are.

What are the things about your job that are most satisfying to you? What are the things about your job that are least satisfying? Are there ways to increase the more satisfying and minimize the less satisfying? A job-needs assessment may be in order!

Take the time to determine what you want and need. The self-assessment exercise below is crafted to point out the best and the least preferred of the conditions of your job. The exercise will help you acknowledge the recognition you receive, the natural expression of you, difficulties you perceive, growth you want, and things that are uncomfortable. You will then be provided with thoughts for maximizing the good and minimizing or eliminating things that need improvement. Taking action is a great motivator and has the power to make you feel more in control of your situation. This exercise leads you into a short-term plan that could enhance your job, here and now.

Exercise: Job-Needs Assessment

Circle the number that most represents your feelings about the preceding statement.

1. My job makes good use of my abilities.
   ① Strongly Agree ② Agree ③ Somewhat Agree ④ Disagree ⑤ Strongly Disagree

2. My job gives me a feeling of accomplishment.
   ① Strongly Agree ② Agree ③ Somewhat Agree ④ Disagree ⑤ Strongly Disagree

3. My job provides the amount of activity I enjoy.
   ① Strongly Agree ② Agree ③ Somewhat Agree ④ Disagree ⑤ Strongly Disagree

4. My job provides opportunities for advancement.
   ① Strongly Agree ② Agree ③ Somewhat Agree ④ Disagree ⑤ Strongly Disagree

5. My job provides the amount of authority that I need.
   ① Strongly Agree ② Agree ③ Somewhat Agree ④ Disagree ⑤ Strongly Disagree

6. My organization administers policy fairly.
   ① Strongly Agree ② Agree ③ Somewhat Agree ④ Disagree ⑤ Strongly Disagree

7. I am well compensated (pay/benefits) in comparison with others that do similar work.
   ① Strongly Agree ② Agree ③ Somewhat Agree ④ Disagree ⑤ Strongly Disagree

8. I have co-workers who are easy to make friends with.
   ① Strongly Agree ② Agree ③ Somewhat Agree ④ Disagree ⑤ Strongly Disagree

9. I am able to use my creativity in my work and to try out my ideas.
   ① Strongly Agree ② Agree ③ Somewhat Agree ④ Disagree ⑤ Strongly Disagree

10. I am able to comfortably complete the work that I must do alone.
    ① Strongly Agree ② Agree ③ Somewhat Agree ④ Disagree ⑤ Strongly Disagree

11. I am able to do my work in concert with my own moral value system.
    ① Strongly Agree ② Agree ③ Somewhat Agree ④ Disagree ⑤ Strongly Disagree

12. I receive recognition for the work that I do.
    ① Strongly Agree ② Agree ③ Somewhat Agree ④ Disagree ⑤ Strongly Disagree

13. I am able to make decisions that affect the work that I do.
    ① Strongly Agree ② Agree ③ Somewhat Agree ④ Disagree ⑤ Strongly Disagree

14. I feel secure that my job will be there and my employment and pay will be steady.

    ① Strongly Agree ② Agree ③ Somewhat Agree ④ Disagree ⑤ Strongly Disagree

15. My work provides me with the satisfaction of helping others.

    ① Strongly Agree ② Agree ③ Somewhat Agree ④ Disagree ⑤ Strongly Disagree

16. My position provides me with the social status I want in the community.

    ① Strongly Agree ② Agree ③ Somewhat Agree ④ Disagree ⑤ Strongly Disagree

17. My leaders support me and back me up—human relations are good.

    ① Strongly Agree ② Agree ③ Somewhat Agree ④ Disagree ⑤ Strongly Disagree

18. My leaders provide technical training for my growth and development.

    ① Strongly Agree ② Agree ③ Somewhat Agree ④ Disagree ⑤ Strongly Disagree

19. I have the variety I need in my work, something different to do every day.

    ① Strongly Agree ② Agree ③ Somewhat Agree ④ Disagree ⑤ Strongly Disagree

20. The conditions of my work environment are good.

    ① Strongly Agree ② Agree ③ Somewhat Agree ④ Disagree ⑤ Strongly Disagree

Your Top Five Lists: Things to Maximize, Things to Minimize

Select five of the items from the list of twenty above for which you circled "Strongly Agree." Label this list of five as "Things to Maximize." Select five of the items from the list of twenty above for which you "Strongly Disagree." Label this second list as "Things to Minimize or Eliminate."

Develop Your Short-Term Plan

Use the following questions to brainstorm and develop ideas for your plan.

1. What can I do to increase or decrease this area of my job, this responsibility, this activity?

2. Are there additional assignments that I can seek to gain more of what I enjoy?

3. Are there unwanted assignments I have that I could negotiate to minimize or eliminate from my workload?

4. Is there a conversation I can have with someone that could have an effect on the amount of this kind of work, responsibility, activity, relationship?

5. Is there a relationship that I could develop that would have a positive effect on my workload, my mix of work, or improve the quality of this part of my job?

6. Is there training that I could take to help out or accentuate this area of my job?

7. Are there recommendations I could make to enhance the environment, recognition and reward programs, or to implement my ideas?

8. Is there something that I could do to make the work I enjoy and the results I am most proud of more visible?

9. What are some goals that I can set for myself and keep visible as a reminder of the kind of results I want and need to increase my satisfaction with my job?

Troubleshooting Workplace Problems

You may be tempted to "throw in the towel" when times are tough and situations build to a level of intensity that seems difficult to manage. It may help to consider that all of the difficulties of your work situations come from past events, from need to take action in the present, and from your awareness of the potential for things happening in the future. Identifying which factor is operating in a problem can help you troubleshoot early on, focusing on key issues instead of spinning your wheels.

Sometimes it is difficult to focus and achieve results when there are too many issues. It might be time to get rid of some stubborn problems that linger because their causes remains a mystery, because a decision needs to be made so you can move on, or because actions need to be taken to prevent future worsening of a problem.

Identify Key Issues

A very helpful technique is to keep problems, decisions, and future concerns visible in some form. The visibility of those issues can assist you in using available time efficiently, keeping mindful of a situation so that you will continue to process ideas for action.

Bob owns a company that sells plywood and other building supplies. Bob has his "big board" on which he daily updates the important business issues he faces. Some of these issues stay on the board for a long time, others come and go. Some of these are "Develop new options for door accessories supplier"; "Discuss employee 401k option with agent"; and "Determine cause of shipment damage to Oregon customer." Beside each issue Bob writes three characteristics: 1. the seriousness of the issue—how serious this issue is to the business, the impact it will have; 2. the urgency of the situation—how quickly Bob needs to deal with the situation; and 3. the growth potential—how much and to what effect the problem will grow if Bob doesn't address it. For each of these measures, Bob uses an "H" for high, "M" for medium, and "L" for low. These measures of seriousness, urgency, and growth potential give

Bob a good idea of the priority of the issue. Every day Bob rearranges the list and reassesses the variables so that he is always focused on the top priorities.

Solve the Problems

When there is an important and urgent problem in your sphere of control, an issue that calls for finding a cause, take action to find the cause. Solutions directed at the true cause of a problem typically provide a more enduring solution. To resolve the problem, you may need to invite others into your investigation, those closest to the issue and those with the knowledge to see the variables of the problem.

When **John** got a position in the product-development department of a large corporation he was surprised to find that the marketing group was a distant entity from the rest of the organization, even through there seemed to be a lot of need for interaction and working together. John immediately could see that things didn't work smoothly between the departments, causing difficulties to emerge from every encounter.

John decided to find out the cause of this disconnect between departments and launched into problem-solving mode. He had met a woman from the marketing department in a meeting, and so he called her and asked to have lunch. The invitation was accepted and John and Murial had lunch and discussed the relationship of their respective departments. Through this contact, John gained a better understanding of the historic source of the problems and decided to take actions to improve communication by using Murial as an ally. John ended up developing a strong professional relationship with Murial, and both were instrumental in helping others to work together better. About five months after John's lunch with Murial, there was a reorganization that brought marketing and product development a lot closer organizationally.

Get Decisions Made

When an individual or an organization is presented with alternatives, it can take quite a while to make a clear decision. Work and productivity often suffer while workers wait for a decision to be made. If one of the issues on your list requires someone to make a decision, take action to make it if you are the decision maker, or do what you can to make the decision and alternatives very clear to the decision maker.

Mary was a project manager in a development organization. Mary typically had more work than she could handle, even with her very strong team of systems analysts and designers. A lot had happened in the past six months, including a major layoff, a radical shift in business focus, and a host of other changes. Mary inherited several projects from another group as work was redistributed. On Mary's list of issues were several decisions about the priorities of projects; several of the projects needed to be slowed or deferred, analysis of costs and benefits would need to be conducted to make the decisions clearer, and expectancies of those that would be the recipients of the systems-development work would need to be determined. Mary put this need to clarify priorities as the top concern on her list, called in her team and representatives of the user groups, and held a brainstorming session to get all the issues out on the table. Her presentation to her senior-management team helped them decide to defer several key projects. Mary still had too much on her plate, but for the moment was feeling a lot better about her ability to deliver what was expected of her.

Take Action to Prevent Future Problems

When you consider the issues that need attention in your job, you will no doubt include issues that you anticipate coming along in the course of time. When you can anticipate potential future problems, you can take deliberate steps to prevent the problems or put contingency plans together to deal with the fallout, should the problem hit.

Jeanette heard about the party aboard a boat that was planned for one of the two groups that worked hard on a major company change. The party would be forty-five days in the future, but Jeanette anticipated the effect on morale in her department. Nothing was planned for her team, which had done most of the development work prior to testing and implementation. The director of Jeanette's group was not one to take the time to recognize and reward, as she felt there was always the immediate next job at hand to get to. Jeanette had a strong foreboding feeling. This issue rose to the top of Jeanette's issues list, and she scheduled a meeting with the director and discussed her feelings. The director took action. The party aboard the boat was expanded to include not only Jeanette's team, but several other individuals in other organizations who had provided considerable effort to the company's success.

 Exercise: Job Troubleshooting

1. Make a list of all of the issues you face. Be as specific as you can be so it will be easier to determine the action that you must take.

2. Analyze each issue to provide some measure of its seriousness to your business situation, urgency of the matter, and growth potential.

3. Analyze each of the highest priority issues to see if you have a problem to solve (Do you know the cause of the problem?), decision(s) to make (Are there alternatives available to you from which you need to select?), or contingency plans to make against future difficulties?

4. Determine the action you will take for each issue, when you will take the action, and how you will monitor the results.

5. Take action!

Make Some Changes

You have more control of major aspects of your job than you might believe! The hours you work, the location of your work, and how your work gets done are key variables that can be more flexible than you might think. You may be able to use new strategies to free some of your valuable time, lighten your load, and add to the efficiency of your work and the quality of your life.

What You Can Gain by Taking More Control

- ☺ Time for family and enriching your life outside of work (health, school, community involvement, creative hobbies, pursuit of interests).

- ☺ Time for training or participation in educational and skill-building activities.

- ☺ Time to take on a new project or responsibilities that may show off unrecognized talents and skills.

- ☺ Good feelings about your employer that can provide you with a sense of trust and loyalty.

What Your Organization Gains

- ☺ Creative scheduling, job sharing, and telecommuting solutions can increase cross-training, staff flexibility, and group synergy.

- ☺ Employees with balanced lives can contribute more energy and focus to the job.

- ☺ Reduced turnover and illness due to stress and burnout.

- ☺ Accommodation for employee needs in this way can build trust and loyalty, engendering a more long-term relationship between employer and employee.

Work Hours

Think about the hours you work. Could you see changing hours to allow you to reduce your commute time, allow you to work in your periods of higher productivity, to be more available to those who depend on you at work, or to better integrate your life and your work?

Ralph often needed to be at his customer's location in the early morning, sometimes requiring him to travel long distances before even beginning his day. He had little flexibility in his mornings. His wife had negotiated with her employer to let her start a little later in the morning so that she could get their son to school, but she needed to stay a little later to compensate for the flexibility in the morning. Ralph decided to talk with his boss, negotiating for a more flexible schedule that could accommodate his need to be with his son. With the installation of some equipment in his home, Ralph was able to complete his detail work in the evening, and this restructuring of his work requirements allowed him to leave work in time to pick up his son.

Job Sharing

Job sharing is a rather new, innovative way to help people achieve more balance in their lives. Job sharing allows two people to share a full-time job, providing continual service or support from a single defined position. Job sharing can result in two people coming and going from a single job situation on a schedule, seamlessly covering all aspects of one job. Job sharing can provide a rich, enjoyable, and synergistic experience.

Tom and **Charlotte** shared a very demanding office job. Tom was the more outgoing, gregarious of the two; Charlotte the more thorough individual with attention to detail and depth of concentration. The comparison of the two was dramatic, and the combination was outstanding. Tom would be at the desk from Wednesday afternoon through to the weekend. Charlotte started the week and would end her week shortly after noon on Wednesday. The arrangement began when both needed a part-time solution. Tom was a temporary worker who took over for the three weeks of Charlotte's 1995 vacation. Tom and Charlotte talked and came up with a job-sharing idea that would work for both of them, pitching this idea to the section manager.

Telecommuting

Telecommuting has become a real option. Fully one-third of all workers in the United States do some telecommuting, with about 4 percent working as full-time telecommuters. You may have to initiate the possibility of telecommuting as a strategy for your job because you're in the best position to understand your job's requirements.

If there is detail work in your job responsibilities, things like report writing, research, analysis, design, preparation for presentations, information management, and other requirements that require attention to detail, your job could be a candidate for some level of telecommuting. If you could establish an office in your home or in a shared office space near to your home and have all the information and tools required to complete work in this site, you could do some very valuable work without having to transport yourself to your workplace.

Laura was being recruited for a job as marketing director for a technology company. The location of her new workplace would require a forty-five minute drive each way—a trip that could stretch to an hour and a half with traffic. Laura liked the job, but thought a lot about the commute. Laura has two children, and she didn't want to give up her time with her children, even for a very well-paying, challenging job. The job was prestigious, just what she was looking for in content and responsibility, and she liked the company team.

Laura decided that she really needed the job to be defined more flexibly. She thought she could be very comfortable with commuting three days and working at home for two days in a given week. Additionally, she would need some flexibility in her work schedule when she did need to commute, to be able to avoid the congestion of the peak commute hours. The offer for the job looked great to Laura from many perspectives, but Laura was uncomfortable with the potential effect on very important family needs.

Laura called the hiring manager and scheduled a formal discussion about the offer prior to signing. In this discussion, Laura was very open and honest about her areas of discomfort and what it would take for her to sign and become the marketing director. The management of the organization looked closely at the job requirements and could see the real potential for Laura to telecommute. Laura was hired with the provisions she had requested and became one very happy employee.

 ## *Exercise: Time to Change*

Look closely at the time, the location, and the way that you do your job. Take time to redesign your job using some of the ideas below:

- ☺ Look for scheduling flexibility. Are there better hours for your work, hours that would help you get your job done more efficiently and in concert with the requirements of your life?

- ☺ Is it possible for you to do some of your work from home?

- ☺ Are there parts of your job that you could share? How would you utilize the hours you could save (life/family requirements, education, new projects, new responsibilities, enhanced involvement in the community)?

- ☺ Put together a plan for discussion and the possible implementation of at least one idea for change to the dynamics of your job.

Make a Move

What are the plans of your organization? What new developments are on the table? Expansion, merger, new business development, new products, or new services? Are there needs of the organization that aren't being met? Look at these changes and gaps as great opportunities for you. You need to be on the lookout for chances to contribute in ways that are exciting to you and that provide you with additional challenge and fulfillment. Try not to overlook your own organization when you feel the need for change. Even lateral changes or a move into new areas where you might need to temporarily drop back in status can help you achieve a far more fruitful future.

You have power and leverage in your own company because you're already on the inside—you are a known commodity. There may be quite a number of opportunities that you can develop to gain much more satisfying work. You probably have a whole range of options available to you from the advantage of your long-standing service with an organization, the credibility you have built, and the relationships you have developed.

Tamara spent years in various positions in a warehouse for a major financial services corporation. She started out in an entry position that took advantage of her clerical skills. As her career progressed, warehouse management took notice of Tamara's analytical and writing skills, and her ability to take full responsibility for a job and deliver results. She became a buyer for the company and then senior buyer, supervising other buyers.

The company began a major project to replace all accounting and purchasing software and to reengineer all processes around these business functions. Tamara saw an opportunity for new experience and asked to work as part of the cross-functional team to develop these changes. In very little time, Tamara became one of the leaders on the team and began working more closely with the systems-development team.

The project took over two years to deliver the major changes in three releases of software and changes to business processing. By the second release, Tamara was leading the effort to define the recommended automation changes, and by the third release, Tamara was recruited into the systems-development unit to become a business analyst. Tamara found that she really enjoys systems-development work and contributed in ever-increasing ways to the major development work of her company. Her continued interest and efforts to learn new skills caused her to change her role and her responsibilities throughout this effort. Tamara has remained in systems development work for the past seven years and she loves her career.

Know Thyself

The key to making successful moves in an organization is self-knowledge. You must know what you like to do, what motivates you, your natural abilities, and the strengths of your personality. The better you know yourself, the easier it will be to navigate changes leading to greater satisfaction. Also, by translating your self-knowledge into language that helps people clearly understand your intentions and desires, you will more easily make your aspirations known to the right people.

Take a Look Around

It may sound strange to you to hear a recommendation as simple as "take a look around." But if you don't make a careful appraisal of your immediate situation, you may overlook the many opportunities available to you in your organization. You may not ask about the jobs of people you work with. You may not know the mission of the various departments in your organization, what positions exist, how they're compensated, and other interesting facts. If you take time to look around, you may find fascinating information and new avenues for opportunity.

You may need to go out of your way to get information about the different opportunities available in your company. The smaller the company, the easier it would seem to find out about the positions, responsibilities, departments, and other organizational components. A larger company in multiple locations may provide a bit of a challenge for your research. Some companies are more open about the different jobs, projects, and career paths in the company. Whether your company is large or small, you will need to take the initiative, ask questions, and seek out information that is of interest to you.

Network Internally to Develop Visibility

It is important for you to let people know of your interests and to show your interest. It's a lot easier to get an informational interview with someone inside your company than it would be to get such access from outside the organization. Ask around your own department to find someone who has contact with people in the part of the organization that interests you. Find a comfortable way to meet a person from this attractive part of the organization and go out of your way to ask them to lunch or coffee, or somehow visit them.

Exercise: Move to Change

If you feel a need for change, growth, or challenge, take the time to evaluate the opportunities in your present organization.

1. Conduct a research project for yourself to identify the interesting facets of your company, including projects, roles, responsibilities, business trends, skills development, and future plans.

2. Make a list of your three top roles of interest (try not to only think vertically—up is *not* the only way!).

3. Conduct research (reading, Internet research, informational interviewing—both inside and outside of the organization) to get a bead on the requirements of roles of interest to you.

4. Make contact with someone in your target area over coffee, lunch, or simply during a short visit to their office to talk.

- Ask for their ideas about how you could develop your skills to position yourself for candidacy in their department.

- Ask for advice on training, reading, professional associations, and other ways to gain information about the role, its responsibilities, the skills and abilities required.

- Ask about internal trends, industry trends, and future outlook.

- Take notes of all discussion topics and actions you can take to increase your knowledge and awareness, to sharpen or demonstrate your skills, and to move forward with your plan for change.

5. Build a plan of steps you will take after this initial investigation.

People Who Make Your Job Hell

Most likely you've met someone in the work world who has had a very negative effect on you. He or she may seem to have a heart of stone; they may demonstrate almost no interpersonal awareness and seem disrespectful to the nines. You may think of them as the bully, the micromanager, the boss looking out for his/herself, the incompetent, and/or the harasser. And yet, you have to deal with this person!

Most of this bad behavior comes out of ignorance. Many people are put into roles of responsibility or leadership without the guidance, the training, nor the human understanding necessary to lead or effectively interact with others. They may have been effective in other positions, but the requirements have changed and they may not be able to cope. Their bad behavior can begin to have a detrimental impact on many other people and the business. The negative effect may not be so obvious from a business standpoint, but will be immediately felt by people who must deal with the person. Truth be told, the bad behavior will have an effect on the performance of all who come in contact with this individual and can be very costly to the results and the mission of the organization. You may need to take direct action to bring positive change.

Some Familiar Characters

☺ There are those workplace characters who loudly and openly challenge or reprimand you in front of others. Of course, it's sometimes necessary to give you criticism about your work, but this communication can be done respectfully and in private. Yelling is not necessary—nor acceptable. Respectfully delivered, you're better able to deal with criticism on the job, clarification of requirements, necessary improvements, and the consequences if improvement is not achieved.

☺ A colleague, client, or boss may act in unpredictable ways, making you and others uncomfortable approaching them with any sort of problem.

Self-confident, competent employees learn successful coping techniques and effective ways of dealing with emotions caused by circumstances, unpredictable events, the moods of others, disappointment, and the myriad other possible sources of stress at a workplace. The unpredictable behavior of an individual comes from frustration and the inability to effectively cope with the conditions of the job.

☺ A colleague, client, or boss may not provide sufficient information to let you know the "why" of your work. Working in this context of ignorance really minimizes the degree to which you can participate using your reason and creativity. You can feel more involved in decision making if you are approached in a way that allows for questions and provides for more complete understanding of why the work is necessary. It also helps to know how the product will be utilized, how the work relates to the mission of the organization, and the rationale for time constraints, delivery constraints, and constraints on how the job needs to be accomplished. You can feel more committed and respected for your contribution if you're given the opportunity to be consulted.

Care Is Required

Try to be extra careful when dealing with coworkers who affect you negatively. Many people have a tendency to respond to negative treatment by accepting bad behavior, feeling that they must somehow have brought it on themselves. You may try to respond to a negative individual using reason and tact, but if the treatment persists, there is the potential that the treatment will wear you down. Most bad behavior in the workplace is unconscious and demonstrates need for development of more sophisticated coping skills. Without mindful awareness and development of interactive skills people may react and communicate from a primitive, protective level.

John was one of the most outstanding people I've ever worked with. Many years ago, John and I worked together in systems development. John added a sense of integrity and qualify to any job he took on. John provided technical guidance to coworkers and had the extraordinary patience to allow people to develop at their own pace and yet give them enough leadership to insure quality in their contribution to our projects. John was graceful in his execution of his responsibilities. He would take an important task, involve others, give all the feedback and information necessary for tracking, and add his unique contribution to the result.

Recently I ran into John. John told me about his present job and invited me to his work area to check out a very interesting project. While I sat with John, talking of our past work and his present-day project, his boss came by. This boss asked John in an angry voice about the location of a letter or proposal. John's face changed, a worried look instantly appeared and he began nervously moving materials aside and scrambling to meet his boss's need. I had never seen John moving about so nervously, so uncomfortably. It took him several minutes to locate the item. He handed it over and the boss stormed off, apparently angered about the response time. Over coffee later, John told me that this treatment was typical from this boss, and that the boss treats all the team members that way. I recommended the exercise detailed below to John, but I left feeling sad. I cannot help remembering John's wonderful spirit as a consultant on many projects we worked on together.

Exercise: People Who Make Your Job Hell

When something happens, and a person you work with treats you in a disrespectful way, try this process to improve the situation.

1. Allow yourself time to process the elements of the interaction, especially your feelings about being treated badly.

2. Consider providing needed feedback for behavior that needs improvement. Plan what you will say and the understanding you'd like to see.

3. Schedule a private meeting with the person to discuss the situation.

4. Respectfully confront the individual with your feelings about their treatment of you. *Note: if you approach this feedback session in a calm, objective manner, and stick to the way the behavior made you feel, you will present a very strong position.*

The conditions of your workplace are critical to your well-being, and your professional relationships are important to your success. Good leaders realize the incredible benefit and increased positive performance that can be realized when people treat each other with respect and dignity. People who make the job hell need feedback to understand the effect of their behavior and to develop the sophisticated skills required to positively work with others. You will need to deliver such feedback to insure this development takes place around you.

Creating Good Work Relationships

You need the cooperation of others to get your job done. Developing good relationships, even friendships, can be invaluable to your career. You meet a lot of people in the situations of your work. Notice whom you especially like, whose company you enjoy, whom you really respect, and whom you'd like to get to know better.

In our fast moving, technology-driven twenty-first century workplace, you might think people wouldn't have time for friendships in the workplace. There is always work to do, new things to learn, action and bottom-line results required. But we are also in transition to enhanced teamwork, strategic alliances, and other efficiencies that will have us rely more on each other, to communicate and coordinate more, to make decisions and take leadership in every position in the organization. We need teamwork, communication, and trust more today than in any other time in the history of the workplace. And these needs tend to engender friendships and trusting relationships in the workplace.

Work Friends

A good working relationship doesn't have to mean a relationship outside of work hours, but it sometimes does. Many people feel greater job satisfaction just knowing that their employer creates an environment where friendship among workers is possible. Friendships and informal relationships are nurtured in a variety of ways at work: company philosophy (bosses who don't frown every time employees stop to chat), proximity (work areas where people sit together or cross paths regularly), shared experiences (projects or sales trips employees undertake together), sports, parties, and other outside events and activities, and similarity (workers who share common traits).

Norm met **Bob** in the first weeks of a major project. Bob was the department head of one of the organizations receiving the new integrated business system Norm and his team would deliver. Bob and Norm had a number of interactions in the preparatory phase of the project and began to build a trust and respect for one another.

During the time of the project, Bob called on Norm to do a number of presentations for his team about the features and benefits of the system under development. Norm reciprocated with invitations asking Bob to present the requirements of his business units. Both would go out of their way to meet in person to discuss issues. Voicing recognition and respect for each other's team was a common practice for both.

When a major difficulty arose that jeopardized delivery of the new system, Norm called Bob and the two worked out an understanding. Bob had been promoted to a more senior position as the project progressed, and he was able to help his supervisors understand the problem and how it could be handled. Because of Bob, a situation that could have been very embarrassing and could have had serious implications, was averted, and the system was delivered forty-five days late to Bob's appreciative and understanding business team.

Benefits of Closer Relationships at Work

- Closer relationships in the workplace engender commitment, trust, respect, cooperation, and support.

- Good workplace relationships can be a source of energy and security.

- When you're of coping with stressful situations, trusted coworkers can give valuable support, understanding, and advice.

- Casual friendships can be key to job efficiency—informal networks in organizations are the predominant way to get the job done.

- You have more influence with people who like and trust you.

Work relationships are a big part of the loss that people feel when they leave a job. And, even though we may not be aware of it, our work relationships are part of the glue that might keep us with an organization for a long time. Work friends can be a source of comfort, support, and care, persons with whom to share parts of our lives and trust with our feelings and thoughts.

Every one of us enjoys the fellowship of others, the sense of camaraderie and the esprit de corps we get from working with people we like. We enjoy sharing our successes, commiserating when things are bad, and having others with whom to talk over ideas and gain new insight. As we interact with others in the workplace, we get to know more about each other and often begin to appreciate the unique ability, knowledge, and insight each person offers, and the care and support we receive from each other. The workplace is a natural place for engendering friendships and trusting relationships.

Downside?

Of course there is the downside to friendships in the workplace, but this can be managed by being reasonable and using common sense. Some people may feel that friendships can complicate working relationships, and even turn nasty. Excessive socializing can be disruptive. Leaders who are friendly with subordinates may face conflicts of personal feelings with professional responsibilities or appear partial. All of these possible problems call for more sophistication in our approach to communication, but do not deny the need for our working together closely, honestly, and with genuineness. If you are sensitive in your building of professional relationships, you will not compromise your professionalism.

Exercise: Take a Step Toward Friendship

Although friendship may or may not evolve, there are things that you can do to enhance your working relationships.

1. Think about a business contact that would be enhanced through a closer relationship. This should be someone you feel can be trusted and with whom you feel comfortable.

2. Define a simple way to enhancing your relationship with this person, fostering a better understanding of each other—sharing lunch or a coffee break. Choose some activity that would allow for some sharing.

3. Implement your idea—invite this individual to coffee or lunch, and allow yourself to get to know this person a little better.

4. Monitor any change in behavior this new interaction brings—receptivity to ideas, extra help provided, increased interaction, an enhanced working relationship? The results you achieve with this person may spur you on to more of this relationship-building behavior in the future.

Most people are most comfortable at work when they can be themselves. You probably prefer to respond to people in very natural ways. It is very natural and healthy for you to develop relationships in every part of your life, and work is a very major part of your life. Good relationships and even friendships in the workplace are inevitable and can be crucial to your success and satisfaction at work.

Downsizing Your Workload

Hold that line! Don't let work consume you. In this age of downsizing and reengineering, there is always the potential that too much work will be available to you, enough so that if you let it, work could intrude on the rest of your life. No one knows your life and your commitments like you do, so no one else can do the job of holding the line for you.

You want to work, you need to earn the money and receive the benefits from the work you do. Work is probably an integral part of who you are. Work provides a venue for expression of your professional self and a way to showcase your expertise and your ability to provide a product or service to others. But you are certainly more complex and multifaceted than the role you play at work. Your many roles could include: mother or father, sister or brother, son or daughter, friend, community member, volunteer, or a myriad of other descriptions that recognize your involvement, your interests, and other measures of the uniqueness of your being. Only you are aware of all the elements of your life, so only you can manage all of these roles to maintain the balance you need.

Roger works for a major manufacturing company that has been downsizing over the past three years. The demands the company makes on each individual have been increasing during this period. Roger has enjoyed his many years with this company, and has also raised a family, helped his father with the family almond farm, is an integral member of his church, and coaches a boys' soccer team. Roger's style is one of sharing, teaching, writing to provide information to others, and building trusting relationships. Roger is a very talented leader, a leader by example, with an uncommon trust and respect for people. Roger is able to accomplish so many things because his inclusive nature allows him to draw on the talents of others in both his worklife and his life outside of work. He has tended to make good use of various systems to keep track of issues, progress, the activities and results of his staff, and projects he must get done.

Roger has always tried to concentrate on the future. He has a very preventive approach, seeking to anticipate problems, and putting processes and procedures in place and in writing for others to follow. His reward for all of the work he has done is his freedom to come and go as he pleases. Nothing gets lost when Roger cannot be around. Roger leaves work on time, takes vacations as he plans, and has often been selected to represent his plant methods to other plants throughout the world. Recently Roger requested and was granted a day off a week to pursue a master's degree at the local university.

Work Smarter, Not Harder

There are many strategies you can use to keep control of the amount of time and energy you devote to work.

- Build relationships of trust and respect with everyone you come in contact with. You never know how a good relationship could serve you and your organization.

- Share all you know and make your work visible to all who could learn from you. The more people know about your work, the more likely you'll be to have back up when you need it.

- Make effective and efficient use of technology. Computer applications can simplify your inevitable detail work, including tracking and reporting information, and other very tedious, time-consuming responsibilities.

- Seek training to keep abreast of the best practices available, new technical tools, and latest strategies and trends. Your continual growth provides new avenues for more sophistication in your approach.

- Concentrate on troubleshooting and tracking the problems and issues of the day to prevent them from growing out of control. Issues left to fester may bloom into major problems.

- Always allow time for concentration on long-term, enduring issues—issues of future vision, mission, and trends. The more you can concentrate on the future, the closer you move to a more mindful, planned approach, and away from an urgent, crisis-ridden mode.

🕐 Pay attention to the balance of other parts of your life—your health, your family, and your many other life roles. To the degree that you can keep the many facets of your life and your being in balance, you will be treated to the great feeling of success and fulfillment.

Should You Work Yourself Out of Your Job?

My goal in this chapter is to encourage you to find ways to get the freedom you need to make choices about how you spend your time. At first glance, the idea of working yourself out of a job may not seem wise. But give this thought some time, and you may see that working yourself out of a job can provide you with additional opportunities and more control of your time. When you can do your job in such a way that you're no longer necessary, you are ready to take on more responsibility, ready for a more senior role, are available to new projects, or simply able to take more time for other parts of your life.

Exercise: Scaling Back

In this exercise, I'd like you to consider that you have your job so well in hand that it could run without you. And, consequently, you now have two days a week available to you to use in any way you choose!

1. Make a list of the roles you play in your life (*father, son, mother, daughter, sister, brother, friend, etc.*).

2. Add to this list other factors of your life (*education, health, hobbies, interests, avocation, professional associations, volunteer work, dreams, spirituality, etc.*).

3. Consider your priorities, and write the top three ways you would spend the two magical days of additional time per week, if you could have it.

4. Make a list of the ways in which you could enhance the execution of your job by "working smarter, not harder."

5. Look at your list of how you'd like to spend your two free days. Now, make a note on a piece of paper that you'll save that represents a commitment to yourself to make time available to yourself by implementing step number four above, and to use that time on your top priorities from step number three. Promise yourself that you'll *hold that line!*

Money Talking

Jobs are constantly changing, and you are asked to accept new challenges as your job changes. Every time you accept a new job, new work, new responsibilities, new assignments, or a new role, you have the opportunity to negotiate. Some of the new work you accept adds spice to your workload, new avenues for expression, new training, new experiences, new people to work with, and ways for you to demonstrate your ability to take on more. When your ability to take on more is recognized and you're given significant new responsibility, your compensation should reflect the change. It is always appropriate to ask yourself how you feel about the compensation you receive for the contribution you make. If you're not satisfied, consider if you're willing to negotiate.

Know Where You Stand, Personally and Professionally

- ⊕ It's important for you to know where your compensation stands in relation to other positions and roles in your organization, your region, and your industry. Investigate salary ranges, position descriptions, other compensation alternatives.

- ⊕ Know where you stand in meeting your own financial obligations and earning what you want so that your earnings are in concert with your plans, your future, your values, and your dreams.

Susan lived in the San Francisco Bay Area, an area with one of the highest costs-of-living in the country. She held an important position for a professional association, one that required her to supervise, market products, contribute to product development, and work closely with a number of senior executives. This position was not initially defined as a management position, but Susan had expanded the role as she became more involved and the key organizational players began to see her worth. Susan was able to contribute in a great many ways. She had enjoyed her two years with the association, but she generally began to feel uncomfortable about her compensation.

Susan found some Internet sites that provided salary survey results in her field, and she set about doing some research. She put together a proposal that explained her rationale for expanding her salary based on contribution, and then she scheduled time with her manager. When they met, Susan shared her feelings about her financial situation and goals. Her manager made some supportive suggestions to enhance the proposal and took the proposal forward to his supervisor. A change that included a new title recognizing Susan's role, and a significant salary increase was implemented a month later. Susan was very gratified with her advancement and pleased with herself for taking the initiative to make a change.

Know Your Options

And what about other compensation? Apart from salary, there are many other benefits that companies can grant that can make your life simpler and more comfortable. These include profit sharing, stock options, health benefits, bonuses, travel, training, child care, vacation time, holidays, parking, a flexible schedule, working from home, added weeks of paid or unpaid vacation, a health facility, professional memberships, and a home computer or other technology to enhance your productivity. These are but a few of the hundreds of creative ways to enhance your compensation package.

Ryan was ready to accept the offer of a job, but called Sylvia, the hiring manager, and asked to sit down and talk about one additional item. The next day the two met, and Ryan told Sylvia that all was fine in the offer letter, which included a move from the East Coast to California, but he wanted to know if the company could also move his sheep and goats. Sylvia was relieved to hear the concern and quickly made the change to include this provision in the offer.

Ryan's story demonstrates the wide variety of needs and wishes that employers try to accommodate. Your needs and wants are unique to you. You may not have a goat, but there are things that an employer can provide besides money that could greatly contribute to your overall well-being.

Knowledge Is Power

The more you know about your industry, the company, the market value of your position and contribution, the benefit portfolio of your organization, and what you are looking for in your life and career, the better prepared you will be to negotiate change. It will be harder for your employer to overlook your proposal if you've done your homework. Often a written proposal focused on your contribution is helpful.

 Exercise: Show Yourself the Money

1. Determine approximately how much money you have coming in each month (income), and what money you have going out (expenses).

2. Develop an understanding of your net worth, keeping a list of all assets and liabilities.

3. Consider areas where income or opportunity are wasted—these may be areas where you might want to consider change (investment of time or money).

4. Develop a target figure of how much money you'd need to make to meet your needs, provide for the luxuries of life that you desire, and allow you to be free of worrying about money.

5. Conduct research to determine the salary levels/income potential for the kind of work you do in your region of the country. You can gather this information by talking to others in your field, by consulting your professional organization, or by searching out one of the Internet sites that provide results of salary surveys.

6. Explore the future potential for income for the kind of work that you do.

7. Identify the transferable skills that could take you into new markets, new industries, or new careers.

8. Consider scheduling time with someone in a more senior position in your industry or a parallel industry to discuss compensation issues—a member of a professional association, a senior executive, or a consultant in your field.

9. Schedule an open conversation with a person in your management structure so that you are very clear about the internal options for increases, bonuses, promotions, and/or expanded responsibilities.

10. Regularly monitor your industry information to insure that you keep your skills current and maintain a clear view of the compensation and salary trends. Talk with colleagues, get information from associations, get information from other sources like the Internet, industry publications, newspapers, or directly from employers.

11. Try to objectively evaluate your compensation, your comfort with your compensation, your potential, and your immediate and long-term options.

12. If appropriate, put together a plan for proposing change, taking on additional or different responsibility, setting compensation goals, and/or making your compensation goals visible to the right people.

Most people are uncomfortable talking about money and other compensation. But compensation is a major contributor to our well-being. It is imperative that we develop sophistication in dealing with this very important factor of life. But remember, knowledge is power! The quality of your presentation is dependent on the evidence of information gathering in your preparation!

Keep Your Job Exciting

Your work is becoming more sophisticated. Technological advances have undoubtedly made their way into your industry and things are changing fast. This speedy rate of change can provide you with a terrific opportunity to get involved and get learning. You will need to keep current on the tools and techniques for success in your chosen field, meaning that there are always new things to learn. This continuing learning process is a great way to keep the excitement fresh in your job.

The Many Ways to Learn

There are many ways you can gain the knowledge and skills development you'll need for your present role or for a role you'd like to take in the future. You can get some of this training through written materials (professional journals, technical magazines and books), online resources, coaching from colleagues or other professional associates, or training from a college, university, or technical school. Be certain to check out the company policy regarding compensation for training—more companies have reimbursement programs for training than ever before.

Finding Your Niche

In the not-too-distant past, people thought of adult education only in terms of standard degrees (bachelor of arts or science, Master's, doctoral). You may feel sorry if you didn't complete as much education as you wanted, or you may wish that you had selected another program entirely. But, if you take the opportunity to look at college, university, and technical school programs these days, you're in for a surprise. New options have crept in over the past ten years that provide new opportunities for you to develop very high-powered, niche skills and training, in a relatively short period of time. College courses and certification programs are available more freely today than any educational opportunities in the past.

Professional Certification

If you want to gain specialized knowledge, develop new or enhanced skills, receive niche learning, or prepare to enter a new stage in your career, certification may be the ticket. Life experience has brought you deep learning that will serve you in business, in interpersonal relationships, and as a team participant, a leader, a problem solver, a craftsperson, and myriad other manifestations of your natural talents. You can use certification to enrich your knowledge and learning, as well as keeping up with new trends and technology. Certification can serve to enhance your professional image and your résumé, while increasing your marketability. Getting certified may be just the educational transformation your need to provide new avenues, new niche training, and new career options. It could also be a strategy to help keep you sharp and current, while propelling your career advancement.

Technical Schools and Extension Programs

Technical schools abound, and most extension classes and programs at colleges and universities are available to you, no matter what educational background you have. College and university catalogs list a variety of disciplines for which certification is available; some of these include accounting, education/training, business, computer skills, systems analysis, e-commerce, facilities management, project management, landscape architecture, marketing, interior design, psychology, finance, photography, publishing, teaching, telecommunications, and others.

Government Programs

Look into state and federal programs to assist you in the cost of certification. The Employment Development Department in your state can provide a great deal of information about programs and financial aid that are offered through different agencies. There are federal grants for specialized training, and you can get information about these programs from the U.S. Department of Education Guide to Education

Programs at http://gcs.ed.gov. A lot of people will be willing to share information with you if you just ask. There is a strong need for retraining our workforce to meet the sophisticated challenges of the world today. Consequently, there's a lot of information out there about how to get the training you need. It is well known that we do not have anywhere near the talent necessary to meet our needs for the next ten years, so opportunities for growth are opening up.

A Retraining Story

Recently the people of a major U.S. corporation were caught up in a major plant closure. The company offered all of those affected by the closure money for retraining. The money was to be provided following successful completion of training, and the company policy was very liberal in the way the former employees could use this money. People were able to use the money in almost any way to gain training that would enhance their career. Funds were approved for a wide variety of training programs, from technology to human services, from business to arts and crafts. Many of the people from this company have sought certification for computer problem solving, systems analysis, programming, network support, landscape architecture, teaching, small business development, various human therapies, welding, process engineering, and cable splicing.

The people from this plant were excited about the possibilities this money provided for them. Many had worked for the company for many years and were ready for change. The benefit offered by the company made those people affected by the closure feel very good about the company and their treatment. This money gave them incentive for change and the means to make that change. Seeing the effect of this benefit to the spirits of those that had lost their jobs was very encouraging. There was added thoughtfulness and humanness to the layoff program of this company, and it was very genuinely appreciated.

Exercise: Learning New Things

1. Look at the requirements of your job or the job you would like to have and identify those areas in which training could serve you.

2. To develop alternatives for enhancement to your skills, or to undertake new knowledge and skill development visit the Web sites of the colleges and universities around you. Go to the extended education or certifications section and take a look at classes and programs available. You can also visit Web sites of professional associations to see what certification is available or recommended. Also try asking senior members of your organization or industry experts in you field about training and certification programs available or recommended.

3. Develop your own training plan.

As you move forward in your career, you will need to continually renew your education and sharpen your skills. There is no limit to the new techniques and processes being developed to meet business, industry, and human service needs. New applications of technology are improving your ability to do things faster, with increased quality, and you will not need to do work better done by a machine. You will be called upon to manage processes, to assure quality, to serve others, solve problems, make decisions, and to work with others in developing new approaches, techniques, products, and services. All of the skills inherent in your work will require lifelong learning and continued growth in order for you to stay aware of trends in your industry and the evolution of your work requirements.

Listening to Your Inner Dreamer

Think back to when you were so young that you didn't know the difference between "possible" and "impossible." Think of the wonderful advantages of the perspective you had at this young age. You were able to dream the impossible dream, to believe in possibilities that might be immediately dismissed by an adult. Bring back this childlike spirit, and you will experience a renewed focus on the positive in your life. You may catch yourself really believing that your goals are possible. Such positivism can be a real asset in managing your career. The spirit of that child can live on in you as long as you question what is possible and carefully nurture your dreams.

The media, technology, and the sophisticated variables of today's world present a great deal of outside influence in your life. It can be difficult to keep on track with your own ideas in a world of "surround sound" information, expectations, and comparisons. Nurturing a dream will require self-knowledge and continual reflection to maintain and persevere. To keep focused on your own mission you will need to be strong, striving to reach your goals that support your deeper self and continuing to be true to who you are.

Your career dreams may be more long-term, enduring concepts that will not come to fruition overnight. It may take years to bring an ideal in to focus, and then even more time will be required as you begin to see well beyond that initial vision to more refined dreams and aspirations. Changing to new job responsibilities can put you in position to develop specialized skills and areas of expertise, exposing you to new colleagues with different knowledge and experience. As you make changes in your career, accepting new assignments and/or new jobs, try to keep in mind the dream you have for your future. Retaining this concept of what lies ahead can make quite a difference in your decision-making about the assignments, responsibilities, and jobs that you accept and seek. Being mindful of your dreams will enhance the progress you make toward achieving your goals.

Cheryl began dreaming of getting involved in management the day she arrived at the company in her administrative role for a large biotechnology company. She was impressed with the knowledge and professionalism of the managers she worked with and wanted to become a member of this team. Cheryl handled clerical tasks but found that she had a very strong interest in the content of the documents she processed. Cheryl began to learn, ask questions, take classes, and before long she was working for the division head, Dan. Dan recognized the strength of Cheryl's organizational skills, her interest in the business, and the quality of the work she produced. She seemed to be able to handle anything that was given to her.

One day a major intradepartmental project came along, and all of the department managers were very busy. Dan assigned the project to Cheryl. She involved people appropriately, made decisions, took actions, and delivered high-quality results. Six months later, Dan lost a manager and appointed Cheryl to the role of unit manager. Three years later, Cheryl achieved a senior management position and continued to thrive and achieve success. Cheryl loves her executive role and treats everyone in her organization with respect. In turn, she is respected throughout the company.

Joe dreamed of working for a major power company in the San Francisco Bay Area and had a friend who worked at one facility of this large organization. In the morning, the crew would meet in the yard and talk before they were sent out on their assignments for the day. Joe sometimes had time in the morning to visit his friend in this yard before work. Joe did not hide his aspirations, and all the workers knew that Joe wanted to do the kind of job that they did. In fact, when the foreman came by, Joe would say to him, "One day I'm going to work for you."

Many months went by, and Joe had been to see his friend in the yard a good number of times. But one day when Joe was there, the foreman came along and said, "Hey Joe, how would you like to work today?" Apparently there was an opening on the team, and maybe because of Joe's persistence, his affable personality, and a few good words from his friend, he became part of the team.

Exercise: Nurture the Dream

1. ***Make your dream visible for yourself.*** Take the time to write down a career dream you have. You can either put it in writing or make a drawing or collage. Put this visible representation in a place where you will naturally see it quite often. *What is a dream you have? Where can you put the visible representation of your dream?*

2. ***Speak your dreams.*** Reveal your dream to someone you trust. Expressing your dreams can provide a reality check and can also help in developing your idea. The dreams you make visible to others have far more possibility of coming true. Most people are basically good and want to help you. And you may get very good ideas and feedback about your ideas and your dreams. These people may offer strategies for the development of a skill that you may find important to your mission. You may land an assignment that could take you further down the path of your dream. Someone may offer to help you develop your skills or experience in some way that can get you closer to the role that you want. *Who would you trust to tell your dream to?*

   There is a lot of value in making your dreams visible to positive, supportive people. When you keep your dreams to yourself you only have one person on your team. Share your dreams with those you want on your team, and you can build more power to achieve your dreams.

3. ***Seek people who can help you.*** Wherever you are in your career, whatever job situation you have, look for people around whom you admire, whom are perhaps in a job that you would love or have skills that you want to develop. Find ways to associate with these individuals and learn from them, to work for or with them. You can volunteer to work for them, offer to help them with some projects, or simply chat. *Who can you identify right now?*

4. *Monitor your progress*. Take credit for every result you achieve that contributes to the attainment of your dream by maintaining a Log of Progress. Set a target of adding notes to this log at least once a week to start. *Purchase a notebook and give it the title "Log of Progress."*

You may need to take direct action to protect your career dreams. Dreams are not always valued in our society and are often viewed as idealistic or unrealistic. It takes courage to pursue your dreams because you may have to take actions with little encouragement. Remember to try to listen to the positive and seek out people who are supportive. Keep records as a way for you to provide yourself with a visible reminder of forward progress. Nurture your dreams—they are one of the most unique and individual manifestations of who you are.

PART III

Moving Forward in Your Job

It's time for you to move forward.

In part III of this book you will take stock of your position in the world of work through the Job Plan Assessment of "Where Do You Want to Go from Here?" You will be reminded of your skills, values, interests, and personality characteristics and then asked to evaluate your level of comfort and satisfaction at this point in your career.

The middle section of this part of the book will take you deeper into the transition techniques necessary for making change. In "What Passion Skills Can You Offer?" you will be exposed to the power of thinking about your skills as transferable to a very wide range of jobs and occupations.

"Your Twenty-First Century Skills" presents several major skill requirements for success in the work world of the twenty-first century. These skills areas will not be new to you, but you will see need to continually develop and sharpen your leadership, communication, teamwork, and technology skills, the skills employers are looking for in candidates who will be successful. In the following exercise, you will understand networking as a technique that is not only a required survival skill, but an extension of your very natural skills and human nature.

You will need to talk to people to make your way to new opportunities and challenges. "Honing Your Interview Skills" discusses some natural and comfortable ways of talking about yourself and your work, providing techniques for taking a lot of the stress out of interview situations.

The final two exercises of the book are devoted to the planning process for making change. You will be invited to craft a three-to-five year plan. The focus of the planning chapters is not the planning process itself, but the quality and focus of your plans. Career plans targeted at developing and experiencing the uniqueness of your being are more likely to succeed in a way that provides fulfillment and enjoyment in the work you do. "Taking the First Step to Put Your Plan in Action" focuses entirely on the first step of your plan. This initial step is crucial to any plan, especially plans that will make change in your life. It's difficult for any human being to make change. You may have thought about change you desire for a great many years, but it's seemed too hard to do. Try to remember that you can never achieve change until you take your very first step.

Where Do You Want to Go from Here?

You have a plan. You may not have a plan in writing that you can pull out and show me, but you have a plan nonetheless. Your plan may or may not involve the place you're employed right now, but it certainly involves the fulfillment of your aspirations—who you are, what you do that is satisfying, the recognition and rewards you seek. Take time to complete the following Job Plan Assessment.

Step 1: Evaluate the Variables

You will assign a score for each of the following questions and statements based on the degree to which you agree or disagree.

> 1 = Strongly Agree, 2 = Agree, 3 = Neither Agree Nor Disagree, 4 = Disagree, 5 = Strongly Disagree

Your values. *(Are your values in concert with the values of the organization in which you work?)*

1. Your place of employment provide products and/or services that you feel contribute to the world in a way that makes you feel good about your contribution.

2. The people of your organization treat each other, the customer, partner organizations, vendors, contractors, and other people as you want people to be treated.

3. The degree of quality that you appreciate is reflected in the products and/or services offered by your organization.

4. The work you do contributes to the quality of your own life.

5. The work you do provides you with the challenges you need to grow and develop in the ways you desire.

6. The work you do provides you with the pride you desire from your accomplishments.

7. The compensation you receive from your work allows you to live your life in the way you want to live.

8. The people you work with respect you for who you are.

9. You're able to respect those with whom you work and come into contact with in the conduct of your work.

Your interests. (*Are your interests satisfied by the content of your work and the field of the work?*)

10. You are interested in the content information of the work you do.

11. You ask a lot of questions about the new issues of your work because you have the interest to ask.

12. You find new ideas and new facets of your work, your organization, and your industry to spark your interest.

13. You go out of your way to find out information about trends, new techniques, and new issues of your work, your place of work, and your industry.

14. You do reading about your industry in trade papers, magazines, books, or through listening to or watching other media.

15. You have other facets of your life that are related to the work that you do.

Your skills. (*Are you able to use the skills you enjoy to a degree that satisfies you?*)

16. The skills you use in the work that you do are those you enjoy and that come somewhat naturally to you.

17. You find that people respect you for the skills that you exhibit in your work.

18. You take pride in your ability to perform your work and get the results you get from the work.

19. You receive recognition and reward for the skills you have and use in the execution of your responsibilities.

20. Through doing your job, you're able to develop skills that you enjoy.

Your personality. *(Are you really yourself at work?)*

21. You are able to present yourself in a genuine way, true to yourself in all areas of your work responsibilities.

Step 2: Focus On Strong Reactions

Review those statements for which you marked "Strongly Agree" or "Agree." Write a paragraph about each of the statements that provides insight into the strength of these attributes in the situations of your work.

Now review those statements for which you marked "Strongly Disagree" or "Disagree." Write a paragraph about each of these statements that provides insight into the weakness of these attributes in the situations of your work.

Step 3: Summarize the Key Issues

Write a summary for yourself of both the strong qualities and the weak areas of the work you do. This will provide you with a fairly objective description of your present level of comfort with your work.

Step 4: Consider the Future

Reread the summary you wrote for yourself in step 3 and then consider answers to the following:

1. What opportunities are available to you for future development, advancement, and challenge in your present organization? Industry? Field?

2. What steps can you take to make your aspirations known to the right people?

3. What questions would you ask to discern the requirements of such a role you think you may want? The approaches to take to prepare? The ways to demonstrate skill development? The future trends that could have an effect on your plans?

4. What developmental steps can you take to prepare yourself for such a position or area of responsibility in your present organization or in another organization?

5. Write down a targeted role you aspire to take. Make a commitment to conduct an informational interview with someone you believe will have the knowledge to share with you about roles of interest to you.

Is It Time to Move On?

You need to be in a place where you can thrive. If you enjoy what you do, there should be enough of this work to satisfy you for a very long time. If you aspire to do something new, that something new needs to be available to you. If you look around and do not see opportunity for you to take steps to develop and demonstrate the skills and knowledge required for a position you aspire to, you may need to move on. Only you will know when it's time for you to move. Only you can process what's in your heart.

What Passion Skills Can You Offer?

You've probably been working now for a number of years. As you have made your way in your career, you've undoubtedly developed some very unique skills. But other people may not even know about those skills or the joy you receive from them. Often the most graceful of your skills are caught up and perhaps buried in the content of your work. These skills may not be as visible as the skills people would easily see from the external characteristics of your role. Others may be blinded by the industry, your technical skills, or the role you play and not necessarily see the skills that come from the fabric of your being. No one but you truly knows what's in your heart.

Marty has been in the insurance business for over twenty years. He has always been recognized for his leadership skills. His true nature is about respecting others and making people feel good about themselves. People always enjoy working with Marty. He took a major risk last year in joining an Internet company, then lost this job to a layoff. He is now being recruited by several top insurance companies. Marty will take a job back in the insurance market to continue expression of his passion for leadership in the next few years. He yearns to express more of his creativity. He loves music and has developed a small side business with his own record label.

Sylvia has been in systems work for almost all of her professional life. She has managed projects and people and has been given excellent ratings for both her people leadership and her ability to lead projects. Over the years, Sylvia has come to feel very worn out in her systems-management role. Sylvia has returned to school to study counseling and plans to become a marriage, family, and child counselor. Sylvia yearns to help people in more direct ways, but in the meantime is finding use of her enhanced counseling skills in helping people as a manager and colleague in the systems-technology area.

Alvin was a pretty good salesman. He won awards and achieved a lot of success in sales. But Alvin has never truly enjoyed sales—he has always seen it simply as a way to earn a living. Alvin's father was a salesman, and so Alvin may have followed in footsteps not necessarily of his choosing. After almost ten years of sales, Alvin was getting very worn out. He found that people tended to like him and for the most part, he believed that his open and honest approach appealed to a lot of his clients. He enjoyed helping people and would spend a lot of time explaining the benefits of the security systems he sold. Alvin has transitioned into a technical position in the company making use of his engineering education. This job pays less but has allowed him to capitalize on his knowledge of security systems. He's enjoying the expression of his expert knowledge and his ability to help people without having the pressure of sales goals to meet.

Two Kinds of Skills

You have a lot of skills to offer, and some are more visible from the kind of work you do (call these "content skills"), some are more visible from the person you are (call these "passion skills"). When the skills you use in your work are in concert with the fabric of your being (when content skills = passion skills), you are in the best position to capitalize on and exploit your unique assets.

Take notice of the way in which the world views skills. You may be labeled by the work you do, but you're much more talented than the labels may imply. A teacher may be valued for classroom delivery and organizational skills, but what about the "softer" skills that allow the teacher to make connection with each of his students? The account manager may be recognized for the big sale to the client company, but what about her relationship skills that provide a framework for trust? The cabinet maker may be recognized for the precision of technical work and not so much for her ability to listen to a customer, understand their requirements, and deliver to meet their unique needs. The manufacturing worker may be recognized for his technical/mechanical skills, while the interpersonal skills that make him a tremendous team player and colleague may not even be recognized.

Imagine the Possibilities

Take a skill you love to express, something you find yourself doing naturally, and imagine how else it could be utilized. Jesse Ventura went from a wrestling career to being governor of a state. When you hear Jesse talk about this transition, he is very clear about the skills he sees as a natural part of him that allowed him to transfer from one profession to a radically new role. Jesse is a communicator, an influencer, and has exemplary media skills. Both careers showcase this natural talent—those passion skills that *are* Jesse Ventura.

Open your mind to the possibilities. The skills that are unique to you have no bounds. You may be the communicator, the leader, the technician, the crafts person, the team player, the caretaker, the teacher, the actor, or the consultant. Your passion skills translate into a great number of potential work roles.

Exercise: What Are Your Passion Skills?

1. Think about five to seven successes you've had in your life. These successes don't have to be an accomplishment at work and can come from any stage of your life experience.

2. Write the story of this successful event. In each case, speak of the *challenge you had*, *the actions you took*, and *the results you achieved*.

3. Ask someone you trust to read your stories and provide you with feedback in the form of the skills they think your stories demonstrate.

4. Look for common threads in the feedback you get from the stories. Look for the passion skills to come through this exercise.

5. Let yourself imagine what jobs, roles, organizations, industries, and/or companies could use your passion skills?

Example: JoAnne told the story of an event that occurred when she was seven years old. It was the middle of the school year and the principal of her school came to her classroom to ask for one of the children of her class to move to another class to balance the site of the two second-grade classes. Although JoAnne adored her teacher and had many friends in the class she was in, she volunteered. When JoAnne told this story, the friends who read it could see her sense of adventure, her willingness to take risks, and her quick decision making. Today, JoAnne runs her own consulting business and is passionate about those entrepreneurial skills that were already evident at the age of seven.

Look below the surface and you will find your passion skills. These skills are the genuine expression of you from the core of your being. You will naturally enjoy using skills that express who you are. You are more graceful in using skills that are part of you. The most flexible and adaptable skills you have are the skills that are developed throughout life and are the expression of the unique person you are.

Your Twenty-First Century Skills

Over the course of both your work and personal life, you have developed valuable skills in dealing with people and things. These skills may be perfectly fine for the work you do right now, but what about work demands of the future? The big difference in requirements for success in this new age will be the continual need for development, upgrading, and enhancement. You will need to be more mindful of your valuable skills and be aware of techniques for taking these skills to the next level of competency. There are four skill areas that are essential to the twenty-first century workforce and will be required of you, no matter the role you play in the world of work. These areas are: leadership, communication, teamwork, and technology.

Leadership

Leadership is a requirement in every position of a streamlined, well-functioning organization and will become even more important. No longer will you see many levels of management receiving and passing information in all directions. You will have the job, the whole job, and you will be expected to provide the leadership to manage your projects and tasks, inform and involve others, and report and market your results. You need to think of yourself as a leader, making certain that you have the resources you need to do what is expected and deliver.

Anne is a member of a department of people dealing with accounting for a midsized food service company. Anne had always been an excellent individual contributor and could be relied on to resolve problems with accounts, conduct research, and document results. She had worked very independently for many years. In a recent reorganization, Anne was given the role of team leader and was expected to provide guidance to others and insure completion of projects requiring the work of several individuals. She found herself calling for meetings, documenting project progress, and identifying and managing problems. Anne continued to be recognized for her accounting technical skills, but developing her leadership skills became what she called "an act of survival."

Communication

You have always needed to communicate in your jobs, but, as you are required to take more responsibility in your organization, the degree and quality of your communication becomes more crucial. You most likely need to communicate with everyone affected by the work you accomplish. You need to communicate with colleagues, enter information into systems, identify and track issues, speak up about problems, and share your ideas.

Juan was surprised when he started getting asked for updates on how his work was going not only from his boss, but also by vendors and by others in the midsized company he'd recently joined. His work seemed very interdependent with the work of others and everyone seemed very interested in his results and progress. Juan liked the attention and found himself developing new ways of providing the necessary information. The questions he got from so many directions made him very aware of the many dimensions and uses of the product he was developing. As his project progressed, he found himself able to explain nuances of the development process and interfaces, describe difficulties and alternatives, and understand how to ask for help and seek necessary resources. Juan felt the more he communicated, the easier his work became, and the more efficient he became in achieving quality results.

Teamwork

The "maverick," the "gunslinger," and the "miracle workers" of the past will not find success in this age of synergy, collaboration, and strategic alliance. Teamwork abounds in every sector of the world of work. You will be required to work with a team, and team skills are what every organization is searching for in candidates. Few jobs allow a person to work alone all the time. Most jobs require some time alone, but more and more organizations are looking to teamwork to provide the diverse perspectives needed to solve problems and insure quality.

Toni liked to work alone and was excellent with detail. In the past, she was most proud of her problem-solving abilities, and felt best when she could be alone with a problem and work it out herself. But after a number of employees left the organization and weren't replaced, Toni found that everyone was required to work together a lot more. Toni was involved in putting together many new reports and was counted on to provide her valuable research techniques to train others. Toni was unaccustomed to being so visible in the company, but also began to feel more appreciated as those she mentored and worked with seemed to put a high value on her skills. Toni began gradually to feel very good about working with others and felt more valued and recognized for her expertise with detail.

Technology

If you are a twenty-first-century worker, you're naturally a technologist. Almost anything you do is assisted by some application of technology, which has provided a means to simplify your work, has removed some of the detail and repetition, and allows you to achieve more in less time with more quality and precision.

Irene was upset by the new technology mounted onto the machinery of her plant to detect trends and provide pre-warning of potential problems. She was proud of her ability to handle emergency situations and enjoyed acting in the moment to resolve problems. Her initial take was that this new technology would remove the emergencies and a lot of the fun of her work. As time progressed, however, Irene became fascinated by the precision and prevention provided by this new technology. Now "emergencies" were the pre-recognition of degradation of processes and mechanical parts in the plant. Irene's ability to understand what was happening when the equipment monitors signaled trouble provided new avenues for her extraordinary technical and mechanical expertise. Irene's recommendations would allow the operators to continue for some reasonable time, schedule downtime to correct potential problems, and make the most of preventive maintenance.

Exercise: Your Twenty-First Century Skills

1. Take a journal or notebook to work with you for a complete work week.

2. Pay attention to the situations of your work and try to make entries in your journal at intervals of no more than every two hours. Log any discomfort you experience in communicating with others or in getting work accomplished.

3. At the end of each day, review the entries about your discomforts to see if you can spot underlying issues involved in the problems you faced. Try to see how the issue you identified relates to potential developmental you may need in leadership, communication, teamwork, or technology.

4. At the end of a week, look through your log of difficulties. Determine which of the four areas of twenty-first century skills seems to give you the most trouble.

5. Pinpoint a training strategy that would help you improve in this area, then develop a plan to implement it.

Networking: Walk Around Research

While you're involved in your daily work, the world is changing around you. Whatever you do for a living, there is competition, there are market conditions, there are trends, and there are technological advances that could have a dramatic impact on your work. You need to keep up with what is happening in your industry, your organization, and in the world at large that could be reshaping the future of your work. Networking is a dynamic technique that you can employ to keep abreast of change.

Networking may make you a little uncomfortable. When you think of needing to be in contact with others, you may understand networking as a formal process or as forcing yourself to artificially interact with people. No one would consider that something worth jumping out of bed for. But if you consider networking something that you do all the time as you travel about in your everyday life and work, the requirement may begin to seem more graceful and natural to you. Every skill you develop will at first feel awkward and uncomfortable. With practice comes grace and sophistication. And because networking is a skill you do already, developing it is really just doing more of the same—only with more focus and effectiveness.

Areas of Possible Change That Could Affect Your Future

- Changes to requirements for jobs along your career path
- Change to the stature and competitive position of your organization
- New inventions and technological advances in your industry
- New approaches and techniques for success in positions and organizations like yours
- Possible mergers and acquisitions
- New strategic alliances in your industry and your organization
- New requirements for your industry, organization, product, or service

☺ New opportunities and potential problems in your industry, organization, or job family

Michele has always been fascinated by the science of biology and has developed a specialty in genetics. Michele has earned a reputation of quality for the investigative work that she undertakes. She has become an industry expert by reading just about everything about molecular genetics, cell biology, and biochemistry. She also writes articles that are published in trade journals and is a member of several professional associations. Michele has successfully maintained her state-of-the-art expertise in a constantly changing and evolving industry. Even though she is a quiet, reserved individual, Michele credits her success to the many people she has kept in contact with over the years. She says, "I would never be able to keep on top of this evolving technology without my network of people."

Avenues to Networking

☺ Professional associations

☺ Industry books and journals (authors of articles, studies, awards, advertisements)

☺ Organizational resources like newsletters, organizational charts, your organization's intranet

☺ Colleagues

☺ Conventions, trade shows, classes, seminars, presentations

☺ Vendors

☺ Friends/relatives

☺ Internet

☺ Formal/informal events (lunches, parties, ceremonies, dinners)

The Power of Networking

Developing a network of professional colleagues both inside and outside of your organization can provide a very powerful two-way source of information, ideas, early awareness, and support. When you share information with others, it will be shared more freely with you. When you keep in touch with others, you engender comfort and trust, and when you help someone out with a problem, he or she will likely be there for you when you need assistance. The more you develop your network, the more powerful your arsenal of resources.

Networking Successes

☺ John was called by a colleague in another department to give him a "heads up" about a competing priority that might jeopardize completion of a critical project component. John was able to find a resource alternative in time to avoid potential embarrassment.

☺ Over lunch with a representative of her client organization, Amy heard about bad feelings of a key person in the client organization. Amy scheduled a lunch with that person, and respectfully and comfortably discussed what turned out to be a misunderstanding that was about to grow to explosive proportions.

☺ Andy learned of an exciting new approach at a conference, spent some extra time with the presenter, and returned to work with a technique that saved approximately two months of development time for a major product.

☺ Loren attended a retirement party for a company executive and learned from the retiree about a new position that was planned in an area that really interested Loren. She followed up with the director of the organization the next day, and inside of a month got what she referred to as a "dream job."

Exercise: Get Networking

1. Take a notebook and label a page "My Network." List your network (friends, relatives, colleagues, vendors, employers, staff, neighbors, members of your associations, etc.).

2. Use the "Avenues to Networking" section above to expand this list or to identify areas where you can enhance your network.

3. Determine the three best sources of developing your network for the immediate future.

4. Make plans to add three new members to your exclusive network in the next month.

Knowledge is power, and the more you develop your network, the more you'll increase what you know. No person can be self-sufficient in the complex, ever-changing landscape of today's work world. You will be far more successful if you stay connected through networking. Stay alone, and your potential for success will suffer. Stay connected, and you will thrive.

Honing Your Interview Skills

When you sit down to a job interview, it may be helpful to think of yourself as the CEO of your own enterprise. As the CEO, you have a much more important decision to make than the prospective employer who's interviewing you. To the employer, you will fill only one of the many roles that must be handled in their organization. But from your point of view, you only have one life, one "you" to give to the employer for the duration of your stay with this organization. So your decision to commit yourself to the organization is, to you, the more important decision of the two parties involved in the interview. Acknowledging and honoring this importance is crucial to ensuring yourself a satisfying work life.

Conduct Research

One of the ways you can honor the importance of the decision you'll have to make is to find out all you can about an organization before you decide to commit to it. There are many resources you can use to research an organization. Key resources include the Internet, directories of organizations, annual reports, published articles in newspapers and magazines, and talking to people who work there or have useful knowledge of the organization. You can call the company and ask for marketing materials, or ask for an annual report to be sent to you if the company is publicly traded.

Get Your Stories Straight

Almost everyone loves to be told a story. Storytelling is a part of every culture. So, when you say to an interviewer, "Let me tell you a story from my career that demonstrates my . . ." the interviewer is naturally relaxed by your invitation to provide a story. If you then deliver a very well-prepared, short, powerful story that shows off the skills that are of interest to the interviewer, you will do more than tell about your skill—the story will feature you in action, demonstrating who you are and how you operate.

An effective format for the delivery of your story is to present it according to this three key point outline:

- ☺ Describe the challenge, situation, or problem you faced.

- ☺ Talk about the actions you took to meet the challenge.

- ☺ Finally, explain the positive results of your efforts.

If you have from five to seven stories "in you pocket"—written out, studied, and rehearsed out loud, you will be ready and confident in an interview. Written stories give you a chance to mindfully choose the words that best show off your skills, abilities, and results. By studying your stories, you'll begin to remember key issues, key actions, and key results. By practicing out loud, you can translate the written word and invisible thoughts into crisp, clear, spoken language. The spoken word is very different than the written word.

Prepare Your Questions

If you have done the work required to know what you need and want from this job, you are in position to ask very professional questions about how the job could match your requirements. If you have crafted statements of your needs and wants, consider these statements to discern the questions you'll need to ask to determine if the job is a good match for you.

Anticipate Questions

There are certain kinds of questions you can be pretty sure you'll be asked during your interview.

- ☺ Most of the time you will be "handed the ball" at the beginning of the interview. "Tell me about yourself" is a very frequently asked question to begin an interview. The interviewer wants to see how you handle such a wide-open question, how you organize your thoughts, and what you choose to present. Your ability to elevate and present relevant facts, provide an interesting portrayal of your experience, and stay succinct are paramount. A good interviewer can discern a good number of qualities from your answer to this question.

⊕ To prepare for this question, you will need to determine the key points you want to present (background, career, interests, philosophy, direction) and rehearse your delivery of this answer.

⊕ In some way, you will always be asked about your leadership, communication, and teamwork skills, and your use of technology. You will need stories to demonstrate these qualities. Craft each story to very clearly highlight the quality you want to showcase.

⊕ Be prepared to speak about the changes along the way in your career—the changes you made, your rationale for these changes, your objectives, and your plan.

Be Yourself

Perhaps the most important idea of all about the interview process is just to be you. Interviewers are interested in learning about who you are so the best you can do in an interview is to be genuine. Genuineness is a quality that people are aware of at a deep level. They may not be able to put words to their reaction, but most people will react to true genuineness in a very positive way. You will be better able to tap your genuine nature if you understand the variables of the work and are comfortable with your ability to speak to the application of your skills, background, interests and results in the context of the job at hand. Your comfort will be clearly visible in your body movement, inflection, delivery, and in all ways in which you communicate.

Exercise: Crafting Your Stories

Your ability to tell a good story about what you've done in the past can reveal your valuable skills and abilities. If you are armed with five to seven stories of success that are in concert with the job at hand, you will be ready to have a very powerful interview.

1. Think about something that you have accomplished in your career that makes you feel proud: a project, a recommendation, recognition or reward you received, a great professional relationship, a high-impact result, or something that was fun or fulfilling for you. Make notes about the story behind this accomplishment.

   - What did you set out to accomplish? What was the situation, opportunity, or problem? Which others were involved? What details provide context and understanding of the circumstances?

   - What did you actually do? What steps did you take? What information did you gather? Whom did you work with, talk with, coordinate with, and lead, follow, and consult with? How did you accomplish each step? What skills did you use? What discoveries did you make? What initiative did you show? What problems did you solve? What decisions did you make? What was your strategy? Your plan? Your driving force?

   - What were the results that make you proud? How were these results perceived by others? What benefits were gained from the activity, project, and actions? What learning or growth was involved for you? For the organization? What feedback did you receive about the results of your good work? What recognition or reward was there for this work? Why was this so satisfying to you?

2. Craft this story so that it's short and powerful, telling the most important aspects of the challenge you faced, the actions you took, and the results you achieved.

3. Hand the story to someone you trust and have him or her tell you what he or she sees about you in the story. Capture their words! They are apt to see the initiative, enthusiasm, analysis, leadership, inquisitive nature, attention to detail, listening and communication skills, or other natural abilities that are unique to you.

4. Change the story to accentuate some aspect of your uniqueness that your trusted person has pointed out. Perhaps the change will be to simply use a word that makes this quality stand out more, be more obvious. *Notice that this story is quite malleable and can be told from a number of different perspectives to show off different facets of who you are.*

Looking Down the Road: Creating Goals

Most likely, you'd prefer to have a good idea about where your career is heading. You probably think about career goals and may have written down your thoughts about what you want. Things change, and it often seems difficult to keep your goals in mind when the world around you keeps changing in unexpected ways. It's possible that your goal setting is aimed at variables that are too open to change and variation. Perhaps you need to aim with more long-term, enduring qualities in mind.

If you set your goals based on your own aspirations, based on your qualities, based on taking the uniqueness of your being to new levels, your goals will withstand the winds of change. Think about the recognition you've received over the course of your life. Make certain that the recognition you consider is recognition that you appreciated, recognition that provided you with good feeling and joy. Recognition that has felt special to you has no doubt been aimed at a quality you possess that provides you with personal satisfaction and pride.

Your Areas of Recognition

Have you been recognized for:

- ☺ The way you treat people, your kindness, your interest in others, your ability to listen and help others?

- ☺ Your comfort with people, your ability to meet people and immediately establish rapport?

- ☺ Your ability to fix things, take things apart, figure out how things work, see new ways to improve things—your practical, real-world solutions?

- ☺ Your new ideas, new inventions, new designs, new approaches?

- ⊕ The ability you have to stay with something for a long period of time, your depth of concentration?

- ⊕ Your ability to formulate concepts, conceptualize the future, see the big picture of situations?

- ⊕ Your ability to analyze complex variables?

- ⊕ Your spontaneous, in-the-moment ability to think on your feet, handle a lot of situations at once, think, respond, and act right now?

- ⊕ Your ability to plan and organize, maintain control, seek order, and focus on results?

A positive response to one or more of the questions posed above will help to identify qualities you have that are quite visible and appreciated by others. This recognition did bring you joy. Joyful experience can be a very precise indicator of unique gifts.

Natural Development of Your Unique Gifts

As you mature, you develop your unique talents, whether you do so mindfully or not. You talk about things that interest you to others and seek out more information about these interests. You meet other people who have unique qualities similar to your qualities and find out through them new ways to experience growth and development. You find people who want to learn from you, and through leadership, presentations, teaching, and instruction you are introduced to new dimensions of your craft—you take your learning deeper. You may write about your experiences through reports, process and procedures, analysis, letters, articles, and other written expression. Through this writing, you find cohesion and clarity of thought and a means to express and capture learning, providing you with the opportunity for advancing your ideas and concepts further in the future.

Take It to the Next Level

You likely want to take your unique abilities to the next level. In order to reach this goal, you will need to be able to visualize how that next level would look. Look around and identify individuals who exemplify the characteristics that you would consider the most graceful and natural expression of a quality similar to your unique talent. From observing them, you'll begin to get an idea about what your goal might look like. The three-to-five year plan you will be guided to develop shortly will target achievement of this next level of development. The achievement of the next level of expression will result in visibility, promotion, invitations, awards, other recognition, and financial rewards.

Achieving the next level of your talent, ability, or craft will result in development of one or more of the advanced disciplines of consultation, leadership, writing, technical and creative expression, and teaching/presentations.

- ☺ *Consultation:* Recognition of your expertise and knowledge as an expert in your field

- ☺ *Writing:* Publication of your ideas, solutions, experiences, or techniques

- ☺ *Leadership:* A more senior role, more complex situations, or leadership in a new area that provides you with new experiences

- ☺ *Technical Expertise:* Further development and recognition of your technical acumen

- ☺ *Arts/Crafts:* Recognition of your artistic creativity and the quality of your craft

- ☺ *Teaching/Presentation:* Recognition of the quality of your delivery, content, impact on others

Exercise: Develop Your Three-to-Five Year Plan

1. Develop a "vision statement" for yourself—visualize and document yourself operating successfully at the next level of expression in your field, your discipline, or your area of uniqueness.

2. Develop a "statement of personal mission." Give a name to your mission (like naming a business), identify the products and services you offer, identify the population you serve (your clients, the recipients of the work you produce), and include philosophical statements about the way you carry out your work.

3. Set up three objectives that are measurable so that you will know that you have achieved the result you were after. Make certain that you have measurable criteria for the completion of the first year of your plan as well as criteria that demonstrates results after three to five years.

4. Document the strategies you will use to achieve these objectives (training, practice, visibility, writing, acquisition, etc.).

Taking the First Step to Put Your Plan in Action

The most important step of a plan is the first step. If you do not take the first step, the plan is dead. Don't relegate your plans to a drawer, never to be seen again. Think of your plan as an active, living, breathing entity that requires reasonable attention and review. When you put a plan together, try to take the attitude that you're always working on the plan. If you are not actively doing something about the plan today, at least some step is planned for the near future.

Jaime wanted to develop her technical expertise with computers. She could see her job getting more technically advanced and found that she had a natural ability with computers and enjoyed working with them. Jaime was in an administrative position but could see that, with some training and opportunity, she could become just as technically savvy as some of the technicians she worked with. For a year, Jaime made no progress—there was always too much to do and training just was not happening. Jaime put a plan together that had a tough first step: she had to have a conversation with her boss Loraine and speak of her goals. Three weeks later, Jaime executed step one of her plan and found Loraine not only receptive, but with new ideas that immediately enhanced Jaime's plan.

Walter wanted to become a firefighter but was having difficulty making the first move. With the help of a friend, he was able to sit down with the fire chief of a small town near his home. The chief provided Walter with information about the preparatory steps necessary to be eligible for such work. Walter left with a plan that he monitored and changed according to his progress, logging his results and moving steadily forward. Walter's plan changed as he went along. He became an emergency medical technician, but he will use this training and experience later as he continues on his quest to become a firefighter.

Chrissy wanted to return to school. She wanted a master's degree in psychology or counseling to provide her with more skill and the opportunity to help people with their issues. Chrissy worked in a human resources division of a major corporation.

She talked about returning to school for over three years before she took the first step of her plan. She went to the department head of two universities in her area to ask questions about the programs offered. Chrissy learned a great deal in those discussions and was able to make a decision on the program for her. Moving ahead, she was even able to secure support from her employer for some of the cost and the time she would need to participate. Three years later, Chrissy graduated and set up a part-time private practice.

Momentum

Every step of your plan is the first step of the rest of your plan. As you take steps, more steps will appear to you, and soon you will reach a point where momentum takes over and you are on your way. No matter how small a step seems to be, it can be monumental to you. First steps could include a conversation with someone, a class, some reading, or attending a meeting. Every step you take invites other steps and provides new information and new avenues for further development of your plan.

Norm believed he wanted to become a career counselor, but he had been in a business setting for many years. He had consistently received positive feedback about his compassionate leadership and his focus on the development of others. Norm thought about changing careers for over seven years as life busied him with new projects and new situations. One autumn day, he finally took the first step of his plan—Norm talked with a career counselor. He then talked with a psychologist, then the head of a program at the local university. He took a summer course to see if he would like the content of the program and he loved it. He continued to take classes, but did not really believe he could achieve his four- to five-year goal of becoming a career counselor. One spring day two years later, the plan took over. Norm was walking along a path on campus and stopped. All of a sudden he was aware that the plan was working, that nothing could stop him, and that he was well on his way. Norm became a career counselor in private practice, and now teaches at a university, consults through a transitions company, and has written a book.

Exercise: Take the First Step

You want to do something important to you, perhaps many things. You want to be recognized for your unique abilities. You have seen people who have demonstrated their unique gifts in ways that you admire. You want to take steps to achieve your potential. You want to live life to the fullest and leave nothing on the table. You want to look back at the end of your life and be able to say that you developed your gift and contributed in your own unique way.

1. What is the first step of your plan?

Throughout his professional life, **Norman J. Meshriy, M.S., N.C.C.C.,** has explored means of bringing greater professional fulfillment and motivation to the office setting. For the past decade he has worked as a career coach in private practice in the San Francisco Bay Area. As a nationally certified counselor *and* career counselor, he has helped thousands of people overcome career-related roadblocks and find more rewarding and successful work lives. Meshriy teaches masters students in counseling at a private university, is a senior consultant for a transitions company, and is a member of bother the National and California Career Development Associations.

Some Other New Harbinger Titles

Do-It-Yourself Eye Movement Technique for Emotional Healing, Item DIYE $13.95

Stop the Anger Now, Item SAGN $17.95

The Self-Esteem Workbook, Item SEWB $18.95

The Habit Change Workbook, Item HBCW $19.95

The Memory Workbook, Item MMWB $18.95

The Anxiety & Phobia Workbook, 3rd edition, Item PHO3 $19.95

Beyond Anxiety & Phobia, Item BYAP $19.95

The Self-Nourishment Companion, Item SNC $10.95

The Healing Sorrow Workbook, Item HSW $17.95

The Daily Relaxer, Item DALY $12.95

Stop Controlling Me!, Item SCM $13.95

Lift Your Mood Now, Item LYMN $12.95

An End to Panic, 2nd edition, Item END2 $19.95

Serenity to Go, Item STG $12.95

The Depression Workbook, Item DEP $19.95

The OCD Workbook, Item OCD $18.95

The Anger Control Workbook, Item ACWB $17.95

Flying without Fear, Item FLY $14.95

The Shyness & Social Anxiety Workbook, Item SHYW $15.95

The Relaxation & Stress Reduction Workbook, 5th edition, Item RS5 $19.95

Call **toll free, 1-800-748-6273,** or log on to our online bookstore at **www.newharbinger.com** to order. Have your Visa or Mastercard number ready. Or send a check for the titles you want to New Harbinger Publications, Inc., 5674 Shattuck Ave., Oakland, CA 94609. Include $4.50 for the first book and 75¢ for each additional book, to cover shipping and handling. (California residents please include appropriate sales tax.) Allow two to five weeks for delivery.

Prices subject to change without notice.